FREDRIC JAMESON

01/22/01

Widely recognised as one of today's most important cultural critics, Fredric Jameson's writing addresses subjects from architecture to science fiction, cinema and global capitalism. His 1981 work *The Political Unconscious* remains one of the most widely cited Marxist literary-theoretical texts, and 'Postmodernism, or the cultural logic of late capitalism' is amongst the most influential statements on the nature of postmodernity ever published.

This volume examines not only Jameson's key ideas, but also the sources and contexts of his writing and his impact in the field of critical theory. With a fully annotated bibliography of Jameson's work and suggestions for further secondary reading, this volume offers valuable entry points into some of today's most significant critical thought.

Adam Roberts is Lecturer in English at Royal Holloway, University of London. He is the author of *Science Fiction* in Routledge's *The New Critical Idiom* series and his science fiction novel *Salt* (2000) is published by Victor Gollancz.

ROUTLEDGE CRITICAL THINKERS
essential guides for literary studies

Series Editor: Robert Eaglestone, Royal Holloway, University of London

Routledge Critical Thinkers is a series of accessible introductions to key figures in contemporary critical thought.

With a unique focus on historical and intellectual contexts, each volume examines a key theorist's:

- significance
- motivation
- key ideas and their sources
- impact on other thinkers

Concluding with extensively annotated guides to further reading, *Routledge Critical Thinkers* are the literature student's passport to today's most exciting critical thought.

Already available:
Fredric Jameson by Adam Roberts
Jean Baudrillard by Richard J. Lane
Sigmund Freud by Pamela Thurschwell

Forthcoming:
Paul de Man
Edward Said
Maurice Blanchot
Judith Butler
Frantz Fanon

For further details on this series, see www.literature.routledge.com/rct

FREDRIC JAMESON

Adam Roberts

London and New York

First published 2000
by Routledge
11 New Fetter Lane, London EC4P 4EE

Simultaneously published in the USA and Canada
by Routledge
29 West 35th Street, New York, NY 10001

Routledge is an imprint of the Taylor & Francis Group

Typeset in Perpetua by Taylor & Francis Books Ltd
Printed and bound in Great Britain by Clays Ltd, St Ives PLC

British Library Cataloguing in Publication Data
A catalogue record for this book is available from the British Library

Library of Congress Cataloging in Publication Data
Roberts, Adam (Adam Charles)
  Fredric Jameson / Adam Roberts.
     p. cm. – (Routledge critical thinkers)
  Includes bibliographical references and index.
  1. Jameson, Fredric – Criticism and interpretation. 2. Marxist criticism.
  I. Title. II. Series.

  PN75.J36 R63 2000
  801'.95'092–dc21   00-032212

ISBN 0–415–21522–6 (hbk)
ISBN 0–415–21523–4 (pbk)

CONTENTS

SERIES EDITOR'S PREFACE

The books in this series offer introductions to major critical thinkers who have influenced literary studies and the humanities. The *Routledge Critical Thinkers* series provides the books you can turn to first when a new name or concept appears in your studies.

Each book will equip you to approach a key thinker's original texts by explaining her or his key ideas, putting them into context and, perhaps most importantly, showing you why this thinker is considered to be significant. The emphasis is on concise, clearly written guides which do not presuppose a specialist knowledge. Although the focus is on particular figures, the series stresses that no critical thinker ever existed in a vacuum but, instead, emerged from a broader intellectual, cultural and social history. Finally, these books will act as a bridge between you and the thinker's original texts: not replacing them but rather complementing what she or he wrote.

These books are necessary for a number of reasons. In his 1997 autobiography, *Not Entitled*, the literary critic Frank Kermode wrote of a time in the 1960s:

> On beautiful summer lawns, young people lay together all night, recovering
> from their daytime exertions and listening to a troupe of Balinese musicians.
> Under their blankets or their sleeping bags, they would chat drowsily about the
> gurus of the time....What they repeated was largely hearsay; hence my

lunchtime suggestion, quite impromptu, for a series of short, very cheap books offering authoritative but intelligible introductions to such figures.

There is still a need for 'authoritative and intelligible introductions'. But this series reflects a different world from the 1960s. New thinkers have emerged and the reputations of others have risen and fallen, as new research has developed. New methodologies and challenging ideas have spread through the arts and humanities. The study of literature is no longer – if it ever was – simply the study and evaluation of poems, novels and plays. It is also the study of the ideas, issues, and difficulties which arise in any literary text and in its interpretation. Other arts and humanities subjects have changed in analogous ways.

With these changes, new problems have emerged. The ideas and issues behind these radical changes in the humanities are often presented without reference to wider contexts or as theories which you can simply 'add on' to the texts you read. Certainly, there's nothing wrong with picking out selected ideas or using what comes to hand – indeed, some thinkers have argued that this is, in fact, all we can do. However, it is sometimes forgotten that each new idea comes from the pattern and development of somebody's thought and it is important to study the range and context of their ideas. Against theories 'floating in space', the *Routledge Critical Thinkers* series places key thinkers and their ideas firmly back in their contexts.

More than this, these books reflect the need to go back to the thinker's own texts and ideas. Every interpretation of an idea, even the most seemingly innocent one, offers its own 'spin', implicitly or explicitly. To read only books on a thinker, rather than texts by that thinker, is to deny yourself a chance of making up your own mind. Sometimes what makes a significant figure's work hard to approach is not so much its style or content as the feeling of not knowing where to start. The purpose of these books is to give you a 'way in' by offering an accessible overview of these thinkers' ideas and works and by guiding your further reading, starting with each thinker's own texts. To use a metaphor from the philosopher Ludwig Wittgenstein (1889–1951), these books are ladders, to be thrown away after you have climbed to the next level. Not only, then, do they equip you to approach new ideas, but also they empower you, by leading you back to a theorist's own texts and encouraging you to develop your own informed opinions.

Finally, these books are necessary because, just as intellectual needs have changed, the education systems around the world – the contexts in which introductory books are usually read – have changed radically, too. What was suitable for the minority higher education system of the 1960s is not suitable for the larger, wider, more diverse, high technology education systems of the 21st century. These changes call not just for new, up-to-date, introductions but new methods of presentation. The presentational aspects of *Routledge Critical Thinkers* have been developed with today's students in mind.

Each book in the series has a similar structure. They begin with a section offering an overview of the life and ideas of each thinker and explain why she or he is important. The central section of each book discusses the thinker's key ideas, their context, evolution and reception. Each book concludes with a survey of the thinker's impact, outlining how their ideas have been taken up and developed by others. In addition, there is a detailed final section suggesting and describing books for further reading. This is not a 'tacked-on' section but an integral part of each volume. In the first part of this section you will find brief descriptions of the thinker's key works: following this, information on the most useful critical works and, in some cases, on relevant websites. This section will guide you in your reading, enabling you to follow your interests and develop your own projects. Throughout each book, references are given in what is known as the Harvard system (the author and the date of works cited are given in the text and you can look up the full details in the bibliography at the back). This offers a lot of information in very little space. The books also explain technical terms and use boxes to describe events or ideas in more detail, away from the main emphasis of the discussion. Boxes are also used at times to highlight definitions of terms frequently used or coined by a thinker. In this way, the boxes serve as a kind of glossary, easily identified when flicking through the book.

The thinkers in the series are 'critical' for three reasons. First, they are examined in the light of subjects which involve criticism: principally literary studies or English and cultural studies, but also other disciplines which rely on the criticism of books, ideas, theories and unquestioned assumptions. Second, they are critical because studying their work will provide you with a 'tool kit' for your own informed critical reading and thought, which will make you critical. Third, these thinkers are critical because they are crucially important: they deal with ideas and questions which can overturn conventional understandings of the world, of texts, of everything we take for granted, leaving us with a deeper understanding of what we already knew and with new ideas.

No introduction can tell you everything. However, by offering a way into critical thinking, this series hopes to begin to engage you in an activity which is productive, constructive and potentially life-changing.

ACKNOWLEDGEMENTS

I would like to thank the following people who have been extremely helpful during the writing of this book: Bob Eaglestone, Talia Rodgers, Liz Brown, Sara Salih, Pam Thurschwell, Angela Bloor, Sophie Roberts and the staff and students on the MA in Postmodernism, Literature and Contemporary Culture at Royal Holloway, University of London from 1996–2000.

The four lines from Noel Coward's 'The Stately Homes of England' are © the Estate of Noel Coward, and are quoted by permission of Methuen Publishing Ltd.

WHY JAMESON?

Fredric Jameson has been called 'probably the most important cultural critic writing in English today' (*GA*: ix). He has an extraordinary range of analysis, which takes in everything from architecture to science fiction, from the nineteenth-century novel to cinema, from philosophy to experimental avant-garde art. This range, allied to a powerful and penetrating critical intelligence, constitutes the most exhilarating thing about reading Jameson.

This study aims to provide a compact and comprehensible introduction to the work of Jameson, and explain why he is crucial to our understanding of contemporary literature and cultural studies. If we want a sense of why Jameson is important, and of the influence he has had on literary-cultural studies, we need to hold two key terms in mind at once: Marxism and postmodernism. For many, Jameson is the world's leading exponent of Marxist ideas writing today; and his work on postmodernism has been the single most influential analysis of that cultural phenomenon. Anyone working in these two fields will almost certainly find themselves engaging with the ideas of Jameson.

Marxism is a system of beliefs based on the writings of Karl Marx (1818–83) concerned with analysing and changing the inequalities and injustices in the world in which we live. It has been extremely influential in many areas of culture and thought, and has had a particular impact in literary criticism and cultural studies: a fuller definition and discussion of Marxism can be found in Chapters 1 and 2. 'Postmodernism', on the other hand, is the term often used to describe the logic of contemporary culture and literature. It is the 'style', or to some people the historical period, in which a great deal of art is currently being produced; a similar use of terminology sees 'Victorianism' used to describe the style of art produced during the later nineteenth-century, or 'Modernism' to describe the work produced at the beginning of this century. There have been a great many attempts to define 'Postmodernism' more precisely than this, and Chapter 6 of this study explains these in more detail. In both these crucial areas, Jameson's work has been centrally and powerfully engaged. His two most famous works are *The Political Unconscious* (1981) and *Postmodernism* (the first part of which appeared in 1984): the first of these is powerful elaboration of Marxist literary criticism, the second a ground-breaking analysis of postmodernism that set the terms of much of the debate. These two emphases of Jameson's work do not represent any shift in interest. As we shall see, Jameson's penetrating analyses of the postmodern are actually only the elaboration of his lifelong Marxist attitudes.

It is as a Marxist that Jameson first came to prominence. His insights derive from and always relate to a left-wing perspective on culture and literature, but he is never doctrinaire, and his appeal is by no means limited to those who share his political views. In everything Jameson has written, it is the range and flexibility of his critical approach, as much as the penetration of his insights, that have won him so wide an audience. Anybody interested in the cultural forms of the 1980s and 1990s, the diverse manifestations of that much-contested term 'postmodernism', will find his diagnoses of that cultural logic essential reading.

JAMESON'S CAREER

Jameson's biography goes some way towards explaining the variety of his interests. Born in Cleveland, Ohio, in 1934, he studied French and German at Haverford College in the early 1950s, travelling in Europe and studying also at Aix-en-Provence in 1954–5 and Munich and Berlin in 1956–7. This Continental European perspective deepened his sense of his own anglophone heritage, and gave important contexts to his readings in English and American literature. He took his MA at Yale, and went on to complete a PhD on the French writer and philosopher Jean-Paul Sartre (1905–80). Sartre worked with the ideas of Marx and of the German thinker Martin Heidegger (1889–1976), and helped shaped the movement known as 'Existentialism', a school of thought which puts great emphasis on the individual's experience of existence as the benchmark of value. For Sartre, individuality carries with it the difficult freedom to choose, and being aware of the burdens of that freedom and the commitment to live with them is the hallmark of 'authentic' existence. Few can achieve this authenticity, though, and instead fall in line with insincere, uncreative roles of living. This perspective is important when considering Jameson's academic career: his own determined individuality, his adherence to a Marxist philosophy in a country (America) that has been at times hostile to such beliefs, even his unique and particular style of writing, are all symptoms of his commitment to an 'authenticity' in the difficult business of interpreting the world and its literature. As this study focuses on Jameson's key ideas, I will not examine his PhD thesis on Sartre (which was later published as a book). However, one point worth stressing here is that Sartre is a figure who focuses Jameson's particular interests: both a literary figure and a thinker in the Marxist tradition. Literature and philosophy are the main areas in which Jameson has worked.

In the 1960s Jameson worked as an Instructor and Assistant Professor at Harvard University, moving to the University of California, San Diego in 1967. From 1971 to 1976 he was Professor of French and Comparative Literature at San Diego; and from 1976 to 1983 he was a Professor in the French Department at Yale University. Since then he has been Distinguished Professor of Comparative Literature at Duke University. But his academic emphasis on French literature should not obscure the fact that throughout the 1960s and 1970s Jameson was writing on an enormously wide range of topics, from Western literature and cultural studies to philosophy. His first book to win him a major reputation was *Marxism and Form* (1971), which includes detailed readings of a number of continental theorists and thinkers in the Marxist tradition. Jameson was one of the first critics of stature to introduce the now influential critical perspectives associated with these figures to an American academic audience; but *Marxism and Form* also includes a thesis of Jameson's own – that critics need to concentrate on the *form* of literature as much as the content, that form is not a mere 'trapping' of the work of art but embodies powerful ideological messages. This influential argument is discussed in Chapter 3. The following year Jameson published another 'critical account' of a school of associated theorists and thinkers: *The Prison-House of Language: a Critical Account of Structuralism and Russian Formalism* (1972).

Throughout the 1970s Jameson published many brilliant articles as well as a number of book-length studies. A critique of modernist writer Wyndham Lewis (*Fables of Aggression*, 1979) elaborated the way Jameson could find interesting and valuable things in apparently reprehensible material that others have seen as hopelessly tainted by the subject's fascism and misogyny; an influential critical position that opens up the possibility of reading *through* the surface of any text into hidden depths. This critical approach was elaborated and exemplified in one of Jameson's most famous works: *The Political Unconscious* (1981). This classic work makes up the focus of my Chapter 4.

If *The Political Unconscious* marks the high point of Jameson's contributions to Marxist literary theory, and remains to this day one of the most influential and widely cited Marxist literary-theoretical texts, then the 1980s saw him increasingly drawn to the phenomenon of postmodernity. An article published in the British left-wing journal *New Left Review* in 1984 called 'Postmodernism, or the cultural logic of late capitalism' is amongst the most influential statements on the nature of postmodernity. Many critics were surprised by Jameson's intervention in this area, because it was assumed by some that a Marxist ought to be hostile to many of the things that 'postmodernism' was thought to stand for. But Jameson's work on postmodernism builds on his rich Marxist intellectual heritage. Jameson published widely on postmodern phenomena throughout the 1980s, broadening his range into films and other sorts of cultural production. *Signatures of the Visible* (1990) is a reading of cinema and cinematic texts. At the same time, his interest in and commitment to Marxist theory and practice did not wither. A study of Marxist philosopher Theodor Adorno (*Late Marxism: Adorno, or the Persistence of the Dialectic*) was published in 1990, and in 1991 the 'Postmodernism' article, slightly revised, together with an enormous mass of other materials, much of it published in journals throughout the 1980s, appeared in book form as *Postmodernism, or, the Cultural Logic of Late Capitalism*.

Since then, Jameson's groundbreaking interventions in the debate on postmodernity have continued, interspersed with more traditional Marxist studies. In fact it is not really possible to separate out these two aspects of Jameson's thinking. *The Geopolitical Aesthetic: Cinema and Space in the World System* (1992) is a critical account of cinema and postmodernism that looks at the way certain films have attempted to embody the totalising 'world system' that Jameson, as a Marxist, equates with global capitalism. Jameson's critical position has also become more global, with interests in Third World literature and culture, although some critics have expressed reservations about Jameson's work in this area. *The Seeds of Time* (1994) is a sophisticated reading of postmodernism and ideas of Utopia; and *Brecht* (1998) is an account of one of the century's most famous Marxist dramatists.

THE CHALLENGES OF JAMESON'S WORK

In general terms the difficulties faced by a reader new to Jameson are twofold: the first is the often complex and always wide-ranging critical context that Jameson inhabits, about which I have just been talking. The second is the sheer difficulty of reading Jameson's own ornate, elaborate prose style.

Any detailed discussion of Jameson's texts needs to be grounded in the contexts out of which they have been produced. This is important for any thinker, of course, but it is particularly crucial for Jameson because he invokes so many and such complicated traditions. This is in fact an advantage of studying Jameson: in exploring his work we necessarily learn about some of the most influential critical movements in literary theory. These movements include Marxism, psychoanalysis and post-structuralism. In discussing Jameson's key ideas, I will summarise the aspects of these critical traditions which have specific relevance to his work. Chapters 1 and 2 introduce some of the key Marxist concepts crucial to an understanding of Jameson; and Chapter 3 engages with the psychoanalytical contexts of Freud and Lacan.

The first thing that many readers new to Jameson note is that he is 'difficult'. This issue – Jameson's distinctive writing style – may or may not constitute a barrier to a reader who wants to access these books. Some readers love the Jamesonian style: fellow Marxist Terry Eagleton, for instance, considers it 'unimaginable that anyone could read Jameson's...magisterial, busily metaphorical sentences without profound pleasure, and indeed I must acknowledge that I take a book of his from the shelf as often in place of poetry or fiction as literary theory' (Eagleton 1986: 66). The critic Colin MacCabe admits that the style is 'difficult', but rather sternly insists 'this difficulty must simply be encountered' (*GA*: ix). Other critics have found it tiresome, burdensome, awkward; Douglas Kellner has gone so far as to call Jameson's style 'infamous' (Kellner 1989: 7). The obvious question, particularly for new readers is: why does he have to write in such a difficult style?

Jameson himself suggests two answers to this question: answers that have to do with *resistance* and *pleasure*. Indeed, these two concepts have a wider relevance than just the business of reading Jameson: they are central to his theoretical approach to reading any literature. In the 'Preface' to *Marxism and Form*, Jameson defends the difficult style of another celebrated Marxist critic, Theodor Adorno, and presents thereby a defence of his own writing. He notes, first of all, a hostility of many critics and readers to a particular type of critical prose which gets attacked as 'obscure and cumbersome, indigestible, abstract'. Certainly, says Jameson, Adorno's writing 'does not conform to the canons of clear and fluid journalistic writing taught in the schools.' But, he asks, what if 'journalistic' writing were a bad thing, what if these ideas of 'clarity' and 'fluidity' actually work as distractions, encouraging readers to skim over texts rather than think deeply about them? He goes on to argue that:

> In the language of Adorno...density is itself a conduct of intransigence: the bristling mass of abstractions and cross-reference is precisely intended to be read in situation against the cheap facility of what surrounds it, as a warning to the reader of the price he has to pay for genuine thinking.
>
> (*M&F*: xiii)

In other words, reading should be difficult: if it isn't hurting, it isn't working. Whether we agree with the assumptions behind this kind of thinking is open to question. We might, at the very least, wonder about a Marxist work which implies that paying a high 'price' for something guarantees its value as 'genuine thinking'; which believes that popular is bad because superficial, that difficult is good because 'genuine' or 'deep'.

But there is another aspect to Jameson's appreciation of Adorno's style: the pleasure to be derived by reading it. 'I cannot imagine anyone ...' he says in the same Preface to *Marxism and Form*, 'remaining insensible to the purely formal pleasures of such sentences'. In a 1982 interview with the theory-journal *Diacritics*, Jameson talked about his own writing in similar terms:

There is the private matter of my own pleasure in writing these texts: it is a pleasure tied up in the peculiarities of my 'difficult' style (if that's what it is). I wouldn't write them unless there were some minimal gratification in it for myself, and I hope we are not too alienated or instrumentalised to reserve some small place for what used to be called handicraft satisfaction.

(Jameson 1982: 88)

The implication is that writing in a difficult style is, in a small way, a radical act. It carries with it the implication that difficulty *is* pleasurable, that we find pleasure in resistance, in engaging ourselves, rather than in simply surrendering ourselves sheep-like to the flow of things. More than this, Jameson says he hopes 'we are not yet too alienated' to 'reserve some small place for what used to be called handicraft satisfaction'. This is an invocation of a classic Marxist idea. For Marx, a worker became 'alienated' from his labour with the increasing industrialisation of the nineteenth century. We might imagine a rural craftsperson making chairs; this craftsperson collects the wood, carves and fits it together, beginning and ending the process of producing each chair. The chair directly embodies the work the craftsperson put in. Contrast this, Marx might say, with the same man forced (by economic necessity) to take a job in a chair factory. Now the worker has only one small, repetitive job – say sticking the arm rests into the body of the chair. He is not involved in the complete process; he no longer finds much satisfaction in his work; and the amount of work he puts in no longer has a straightforward relationship with the finished product. In all he has become *alienated* from his labour. Jameson's use of 'alienated' here suggests, without actually saying it, that he is like the old-fashioned craftsperson: that his writing is individual, unique, it has quirks and rough edges that reflect his own investment of labour in it. This is set in opposition to the mass-produced product, the machine-tooled writing that is free from the rough edges, but lacks the humanity. It is an appealing model, but we can suggest at least tentatively that it is not the *only* way in which we might think of the Jamesonian style.

We might, for instance, think of Jameson as a highly respected and highly paid part of the critical-academic machine, an industry that

earns billions of dollars each year in America alone by selling education. We might see Jameson's stylistic difficulty as a means of repelling
the ignorant and the working classes and of speaking only to those who
have the expensive education (which Jameson's profitable industry
continues to offer for sale) to enable them to understand. Just as we
are encouraged by capitalism to value our belongings because we had
to spend a lot of money on them, we might be encouraged to value
Jameson's difficulty because we have had to spend tens of thousands of
dollars on the education that enables us to understand it. On this
model, a strategy such as the *Routledge Critical Thinkers* series that
provides a cut-price access to this material could be thought of as the
more radical approach.

Looking at an example of the Jamesonian sentence might help
pinpoint some of these issues. Chapter 3 of *The Political Unconscious*
looks at 'the novel', and reads the French novelist Honore de Balzac to
illustrate his case. Near the beginning of the chapter, Jameson writes:

> Indeed, as any number of 'definitions' of realism assert, and as the totemic
> ancestor of the novel, *Don Quixote*, emblematically demonstrates, that
> processing operation variously called narrative mimesis or realistic represen-
> tation has as its historic function the systematic undermining and
> demystification, the secular 'decoding' of those preexisting inherited tradi-
> tional or sacred narrative paradigms which are its initial givens.[1]

> 1   See in particular Roman Jakobson, 'On Realism in Art,' in K. Pomorska
>   and L. Matejka, eds., *Readings in Russian Formalist Poetics* (Cambridge:
>   MIT Press, 1971), pp. 38–42. 'Decoding' is a term of Deleuze and Guattari:
>   see the *Anti-Oedipus*, pp. 222–228.]

(The Political Unconscious: 152)

What sort of pleasure do we derive from reading a sentence such as
this? Or, to put the question another way, we could ask what pleasure
would be *lost* had Jameson written something like this: 'Novels, from
Don Quixote onwards, that have attempted a "realistic representation" of
things have not in fact been doing this, they have actually been undermining and "decoding" the ancient sacred narratives on which they are
distantly based.' Jameson might say that by forcing me to ponder suffi-
ciently to come up with my reduction of his sentence he has done his
job; he has made me think. But there is also a danger that I might have

been too baffled even to begin this process of thinking through, or that I might give up reading the sentence and turn instead to the shallow 'cheap' writing he elsewhere denigrates. 'Thinking' in this idiom is not a natural activity, as Jameson himself might say.

The sentence I have quoted here illustrates a second feature of the 'Jamesonian' style. This sentence, with its pendant footnote, positions itself in a network of other critical thinkers and works, so much so that we cannot hope to grasp what Jameson is going on about unless we also glance at Jakobson, Pomorska, Matejka, Deleuze and Guattari. If we think of this as an excellent way of reminding the reader that nothing can be understood in isolation, we also need to consider the ways it broadcasts a certain implicit value. Professor Jameson has had time, and is clever enough, to have read and understood all these people. If his readers have not, even the brightest might come away from the work feeling stupid. This positions the reader in effect as the inferior, and Jameson (and his ideal reader) as superior. The very structure of the sentence contributes to this. It starts with a subject clause that is easy to follow ('as any number of "definitions" of realism assert…'), but then introduces a subordinate clause ('and as the totemic…emblematically demonstrates') that we have to hold over until we have reached the main verb ('has') so that we can understand exactly what has been asserted or demonstrated. The subject of the sentence ('that processing operation variously called narrative mimesis or realistic representation') is unwieldy, and begs a number of questions (What is it processing? What is the distinction between narrative mimesis and realistic representation?), but again it needs to be mentally shelved, to be held over in the reader's mind until the sentence as a whole has revealed itself. The main verb ('…has…') is itself qualified ('as its historic function') and the object is a lengthy tail that lists a variety of items ('the systematic undermining', 'demystification', 'the secular "decoding"' of 'those pre-existing inherited traditional (narrative paradigms)' 'or sacred narrative paradigms' 'which are its initial givens'). The process of understanding all this, then, involves a lengthy exercise of breaking down the elements and then working out how they relate to one another. The ideal reader will need a particularly capacious brain in which to hold all these thoughts. 'Lesser' readers may have lost the thread before they come to the full stop; they (or we) will have to re-read, and possibly re-re-read. If Jameson is encouraging us to re-re-read everything he writes, then he is flirting with the danger that many people will lose patience and simply give up. On the other hand, there is the possibility that the 'pleasure' to be derived from reading a sentence like this is a sort of egoistic self-congratulation that I, the reader, *have understood something difficult*. The passage continues:

> The 'objective' function of the novel is thereby also implied: to its subjective and critical, analytic, corrosive mission must now be added the task of producing as though for the first time that very life world, that very 'referent' — the newly quantifiable space of extension and market equivalence, the new rhythms of measurable time, the new secular and 'disenchanted' object world of the commodity system, with its post-traditional daily life and its bewilderingly empirical, 'meaningless,' and contingent *Umwelt* — of which this new narrative discourse will then claim to the 'realistic' reflection.

(*PU*: 152)

I am not going to break down this sentence element by element as I did above, but we can note one or two things about it. For starters, there is Jameson's habit of placing certain terms inside quotation marks. This has the effect of making the reader think twice about the term used. This in turn introduces another aspect of Jamesonian stylistics. As we shall see in Chapter 2, it is a central feature of Jameson's criticism that the attentive reader needs to pay as much attention to the *form* of literary texts as to the *content*. By deliberately making his writing prickly and indigestible, Jameson is calling attention to the form of his own writing. In effect he is saying that his writing is not a transparent window onto the subject of his essays, but is a part of the way his essays produce their meaning; and that by extension all writing (whether it admits it or not) is like this. This is a variation of the 'resistance' reading of Jameson I mentioned earlier. Picking two sentences and dissecting them like this clearly doesn't do justice to the overall effect of reading Jameson. In a sense doing what I have just done, resisting in this way, entirely justifies Jameson's technique; this is writing that has not slipped easily down; it has exercised my intellect.

THIS BOOK

The following chapters examine Jameson's key ideas. They are arranged chronologically to give a clear impression of the ways in which he has developed and extended a rich theoretical tradition. This is followed by a chapter entitled 'After Jameson' which explores the impact Jameson has had on the worlds of criticism, theory and philosophy. Throughout the book I refer to Jameson's works using abbreviations, such as *PU* for *The Political Unconscious*. A full list of these abbreviations is found in the first part of the 'Further Reading' section, which lists and comments on Jameson's own works. The second part of this section suggests other studies of Jameson which might be useful. Wherever I quote a critic, his or her name and the date of the work will appear after the citation, and full details of these works can be found in the 'Works Cited' section which follows Further Reading.

Reading Jameson is never less than stimulating, and at his best he is one of the most exciting and penetrating critics writing today. His are some of the most brilliant developments in the traditions of Marxist criticism, and his insights into the whole range of contemporary cultural life are marvellous.

KEY IDEAS

1

MARXIST CONTEXTS

Jameson is first and foremost a Marxist thinker, and the bulk of his work has directly or indirectly engaged with the traditions of Marxist thinking in the twentieth century. Some of his books have functioned as both primers in and critiques of the major Marxist philosophers: *Marxism and Form* (1971) was, for many American readers, the first serious work of scholarship to introduce them to the important Marxist critics Theodor Adorno (1903–69), Walter Benjamin (1892–1940), and Georg Lukacs (1885–1971). *The Political Unconscious* (1980) includes lengthy discussions of the Marxism of Louis Althusser (1918–90), amongst others. The more complex *Late Marxism* (1990) remains one of the most sophisticated and challenging analysis of Theodor Adorno's writing we have. The best way to read both of these books is to have some sense of the terms of the Marxist debate, and that is what this chapter sets out to provide.

Before embarking on that project, though, it is worth touching on one key issue to which we will return. Karl Marx's writings and theories have been debated and discussed by a great many people, and there are various sometimes conflicting interpretations of what he is saying. Jameson can be positioned within these currents of debate, as can any Marxist, but it is worth saying *why* it is worthwhile doing so: Jameson himself early in *The Political Unconscious* advises readers to 'pass over at once' the first chapter if they are uninterested in the internal debates of Marxist criticism (*PU*: 23). Yet without some understanding of the ways Marxist thought have developed since the days of Marx it is not possible to have a thorough sense of just how significant Jameson's own interventions in those debates have been. It is also worthwhile admitting my own positions in these debates, because my own biases are liable to shape my account of Jameson's position. The most significant contested area with which Jameson's Marxism can be identified has to do with the issue of *totality*. To use the jargon, there are Marxists who are called 'Hegelian' after the nineteenth-century German philosopher Georg Hegel (1770–1831), and who believe that we need to understand the whole picture, the entire system as a totality; there are also Marxists sometimes called 'Althusserian' after the twentieth-century French thinker Louis Althusser (1918–90), who consider this sort of 'totalising' oppressive. If this seems a little obscure, then the terms are explained below in more detail, after a brief elaboration of certain key Marxist concepts. It is worth noting, however, that Jameson is usually seen as a Hegelian Marxist, an inheritor of the traditions of Lukacs and Adorno and more or less hostile to an Althusserian approach. My own position is more Althusserian, which partly explains why I detail Althusser's contributions to the debate here; but I should also add that it seems to me that Jameson is a much more Althusserian thinker than he is usually seen as being. This discussion is crucial to an understanding of many of Jameson's works, but it also has acute relevance to his entry into the debates on postmodernism in the 1980s. Many were surprised that a thinker so wedded to ideas of 'totality' should have been so deeply engaged with the phenomenon of postmodernism, which is (amongst many other things) characterised by a distrust of 'the whole picture' and a love of fragmentation and dislocation. This is something I deal with in more detail in Chapter 6; at the moment it is enough to acknowledge that Jameson's Marxism is not so straightforward as a 'traditional Hegelianism'. In what follows I have held over more detailed discussion of Jameson's debts to Lukacs and Adorno to Chapter 3, where they can be keyed to more specific accounts of *Marxism and Form* and *Late Marxism*.

MARX

Karl Marx (1818–83) was a critic of political economy and a philosopher whose analyses of what he called 'Capitalism' have proved enormously influential. For most of the twentieth century, many millions of people have lived under regimes that claimed to be derived from his teachings, and it can be hard to separate out what Marx wrote and theorised from the baleful manner in which his ideas have been put into practice all around the world. With the collapse of the Berlin Wall, there has been a sense that 'Marxism' has now been discredited, which, if it were true, would make a thinker like Jameson nothing more than an out-of-date curio. But 'Marxism' is something very different from the reductive political programmes that have been derived from Marx's writings; as he himself said in later life, to his collaborator Friedrich Engels (1820–95) 'all I know is that I am not a Marxist'.

The crucial point about Marx's philosophy is that it is a *materialist* philosophy, which is to say rather than being concerned with philosophical abstracts like 'truth', 'beauty', 'spirit', and the like, it is always concerned with the actual world in which people live and, more specifically, has engaged in an attempt to make the world a better place in which to live. 'The philosophers,' Marx wrote in 1845, 'have only *interpreted* the world in various ways; the point is to *change* it' (Marx: 158). The world needs to be changed, according to Marx, because society is inequitable and oppressive, and millions live in misery and poverty when they need not do so. Philosophers, he argues, ought to work out why society works so badly to be able to suggest ways to make it work better, and in order to do that they need to determine the organising principle behind society. Marx was very clear on what he thought this organising principle was: economics. In the preface (for instance) to his monumental analysis of capitalism, called *Capital*, he declares 'his ultimate aim…to lay bare the economic law of motion of modern society'. In *The German Ideology* he describes his proposed alternative to capitalism in these terms: 'Communism differs from all previous movements in that it overturns the basis of all earlier relations of production and intercourse, and for the first time consciously treats all natural premises as the creatures of men…its organisation is, therefore, essentially economic.' Clearly, there is a lot more to society and culture than just economics, but Marx believed that all the things we observe in human life, from poverty and wealth to religion, art, politics, and even sport, are all *determined* by the economic relations between people. 'Determined' means that these things derive from economic roots, so that if you analyse them in enough depth you will eventually discover that they are the expression of underlying economic relations. For example, a priest in a religion might claim to have nothing to do with economics or politics but instead to be focused on spiritual things; but Marx argued that this was just a kind of smoke-screen. Religion, Marx thought, was designed to distract people from the miseries of their life, to stop the working classes rising up against the injustices of the world by indoctrinating them into obeying authority (with 'God' as the ultimate authority figure) and by prom-ising a better life after death (so that they wouldn't rock the boat in *this* life). In this respect Marx thought all religions were like a drug, stupe-fying the populace – 'religion' as he famously remarked, 'is the opium of the people' (Marx: 115). So, although religion doesn't admit this on the surface, its real nature is determined by economics, or more precisely by the need to make capitalism work more smoothly.

Although Marx wrote little by way of literary or cultural criticism, we can see how the same principle might be applied to art. All art grows out of economic realities: artists are real people who live out economic relations with other people. Some art tries to disguise this basic fact, and creates an imaginary universe in which these economic factors – class, money, oppression, and so on – miraculously do not apply. Other art – for some Marxists, *better* art – makes people aware of the realities of society. The point is that, for Marx, the root of all human behaviour was in the way the different classes, and in particular the middle classes or bourgeoisie on the one hand and the working classes on the other, have competed for money, or, in economic terms, for the 'means of production', for the factories and resources that create wealth.

BASE, SUPERSTRUCTURE AND IDEOLOGY

The model Marx developed to express these relations in society was that of *base and superstructure*. The 'base' of all societies, according to Marx, is economic: baldly, it is all about money and who owns the means to make money. Out of this base grows or is constructed a 'superstructure' that is 'determined' by this base. In other words, the shape the 'superstructure' takes always depends upon the shape of the base. The 'superstructure' consists of things like the forms of law and political representation of the society: so, for example, an economic base that is all about private property and owning things is going to produce a superstructural set of laws that are primarily designed to protect property. But the superstructure also includes things like religion, ethics, art and culture, which is one reason why Marxist theory has been so influential in literary studies. These are things that Marx defined with a term crucial to an understanding of Jameson: *ideology*.

IDEOLOGY

For Marx, 'ideology' was 'false consciousness', a set of beliefs that obscured the truth of the economic basis of society and the violent oppression that capitalism necessarily entails. Various people believe various things: for instance that the fact that some people are rich and some people poor is 'natural and inevitable'; or that black people are inferior. The purpose of these beliefs, according to Marx, is to obscure the truth. People who believe these things are not going to challenge or even recognise the inequalities of wealth in society, and so are not going to want to change them. For Marx, the task was clear: to disabuse people of their 'false consciousnesses' so that they could see the injustices of society for what they are – both appalling and curable. Subsequent Marxist thinkers have refined Marx's original simple conception of 'ideology', and the term has become increasingly important in Marxist literary theory. Ideology becomes the system of ideas by which people structure their experience of living in the world; this is not something straightforwardly 'right' or 'wrong', but rather a complex network of relations and attitudes. 'Ideology', then, includes both obviously 'wrong' systems of thought like racism, but also more complex aesthetic and cultural responses. The decision to drink Pepsi rather than Coke is ideological in a Marxist sense because it is shaped by some significant economic forces (both companies have a lot of money invested in trying to persuade you to do one or the other); but clearly the preference for Pepsi is not 'wrong' in the same way that racism is wrong. A contemporary critique of ideology like Jameson's is less concerned with identifying right and wrong, and more interested in teasing out the ways culture and art affect and even construct individuals' sense of themselves. In the words of Louis Althusser, ideology is seen more as 'a "representation" of the imaginary relationship of individuals to their real conditions of existence' (Althusser: 155). It is no longer possible simply to step outside ideology and see it as false; Jameson understands that all of the terms in which we understand our existence are 'already soaked and saturated in ideology' (*GA*: 2). Whether we think of ourselves as family members (daughters, sisters, and so on), as 'citizens', as 'workers' (which is to say, whether it is our job that most importantly defines who we are for ourselves), as 'students', as 'music-lovers' or 'sportswomen', or whatever – in all these cases, and in any others we could name, these categories (family, work, leisure) have already been defined by ideology in a complex relationship with the economic dynamics of late capitalism.

For French Marxist critic Louis Althusser, 'ideology' was in some senses a more important tool of the state than the more conventionally recognised 'Repressive State Apparatuses' like the army and the police. This applies in the sense that (for instance) convincing people to *believe* that they shouldn't go on strike is much more effective than sending in armed police to break up a strike that has already happened. For Althusser, various 'Ideological State Apparatuses' or 'ISAs' infiltrate our consciousness from the very beginning: he identifies the educational ISA (school and college, which teach us to think in a certain way), the family ISA (which means that merely being born into the standard family conditions our thought), the legal ISA, the political ISA, the trade union ISA, the communications ISA and the cultural ISA (Althusser: 151). If we wanted an example of how this works, we might want to look back at pre-democracy South Africa. South Africa used to be a very repressive state, where a small minority of white people kept the vast majority of black people in disenfranchised poverty. To keep this power, the South African state employed the 'Repressive State Apparatuses' that Althusser talks about: a brutal, well-armed police force, prisons, torture, and so on. But they also deployed a great many 'Ideological State Apparatuses' that were designed to convince black South Africans that they had no *right* to be unhappy about the misery in which they lived because they were inferior, and simultaneously to justify white South Africans in the belief that *they* were superior. Educational ISAs taught a particular narrative of South African history, in which white settlers brought 'civilisation' to a barbarous black country; the legal ISAs for many years sharply distinguished between white and black human beings; political ISAs gave black South Africans spurious representation in parliaments without real power; communications ISAs like the news tended to concentrate on crime and unrest committed by blacks, creating a climate of opinion that black South Africans were dangerous and needed to be controlled; and cultural ISAs in the form of TV, cinema, novels and other art, valorised whiteness, buying into, for instance, a 'white' model of beauty, which is still lamentably widely prevalent in today's Western cultures, that was opposed to a model of black 'ugliness'. None of these things were as obviously violent as a South African police truncheon coming down on somebody's head, but they contributed just as effectively to a culture of violent oppression. A Marxist critic would insist that any cultural text produced in these historical and political contexts needs to be read as ideological.

This attitude to 'ideology' and the 'superstructure' has profoundly shaped the Marxist traditions of literary and cultural criticism. As Jameson points out, as early as the 1930s Theodor Adorno was appropriating the whole of culture to an analysis of 'ideology' in this extended sense. Culture, says Jameson, is 'to be thought of as something more and other than...the false consciousness, that we associate with the word ideology', and is instead something that possesses an 'uneasy existence, an uncertain status':

> Adorno's treatment of these cultural phenomena – musical styles as well as philosophical systems, the hit parade along with the nineteenth-century novel – makes it clear that they are to be understood in the context of what Marxism calls the *superstructure*.... [Such criticism] presupposes a movement from the intrinsic to the extrinsic in its very structure, from the individual fact or work toward some larger socio-economic reality behind it.
>
> (M&F: 4)

Whilst this does not mean that a reading of (say) Jane Austen's *Pride and Prejudice* or George Lucas's *Star Wars* can be completely reduced to a reading of the 'socio-economic' conditions behind them, it does imply that a reading that missed out the 'base' would be deficient. It also suggests that *critics* – people who, like Jameson, spend their time 'reading' the texts and artefacts of culture like books and films – can perform a useful Marxist critique of society by analysing the way in which culture operates to establish and maintain ideological relations within society.

Some early Marxist critics worked with the 'base-superstructure' model in a way that more recent thinkers have often seen as rather unsophisticated – the label 'vulgar Marxism' is sometimes applied to thinkers who apply this more old-fashioned version of Marxist thought. For a vulgar Marxist the relationship between base and super-structure is very straightforward: an oppressive base produces oppressive culture, in which only a few individuals – people who delib-erately struggle to produce art that resists the aesthetic consensus of the age – are able to transcend. More recent Marxism, however, has seen the relationship between culture and society in much more complex terms; and in particular it has turned away from imagining that there is a simple *causal* relationship between base and superstruc-ture. A key figure in this newer development in Marxist theory is Louis Althusser. Althusser (1918–90) was a French philosopher and academic, whose own troubled life – he strangled his wife and ended his days in a lunatic asylum – has sometimes overshadowed the great significance of his thinking. Althusser started writing at a time, the early 1960s, when the excesses of Stalinist dictatorship in the nomi-nally 'communist' Soviet Union had done much to discredit Marxism as a political philosophy; what he did was to re-read and revivify what Marx's actual writings were rather than what other people had made of Marx.

ALTHUSSER AND TOTALITY

Althusser brought to his reading of Marx a mistrust of 'totalities', of ways of looking at the world in terms of its entirety or wholeness. In various articles and books of criticism he argued that Marxism needed to be purged of Hegelianism. This might seem a difficult project, because everybody agrees that Marx was profoundly influenced by the great German idealist philosopher, Georg Wilhelm Friedrich Hegel (1770–1831), to the extent that many thinkers have seen Marxism as nothing more than a version of Hegel's political ideas applied to the material world. Many key Marxist concepts, such as the dialectic, are undeniably adopted directly from Hegel.

DIALECTICS

The word 'dialectics' derives from the Greek word for argument or debate, and refers to a particular method of doing philosophy by stating a proposition (a *thesis*), then examining its contrary or opposite to see whether it has anything valid to contribute to the debate (the *antithesis*), and finally arriving at a third proposition that incorporates both sides (the *synthesis*). The following, admittedly banal, example embodies a dialectical approach: *Thesis*: 'All crows are black.' *Antithesis*: 'On the contrary, there is a small number of crows who suffer from albinism and are white.' *Synthesis*: '*Most* crows are black.' The word was originally associated with the ancient Greek philosophers Socrates and Plato, whose philosophical works take the form of dialogues where cases are developed dialectically. Whilst many philosophers have seen the roundedness of the dialectical method as preferable to mere assertion, some – like Hegel, whose name is particularly associated with the terms 'thesis' 'antithesis' and 'synthesis' used above – have elevated the dialectic to a sort of universal principle. Hegel saw history as a totality in which a vague and mystically conceived universal spirit (something like a version of God) worked out various conflicts and contradictions in the world before arriving at a tremendous resolution. Another way of conceptualising the Hegelian dialectic would be to see the *ideal* and the *real* as thesis and antithesis – so 'justice' is an abstract ideal, and might be opposed to 'the law' which is often accused of being unjust. But unless it is embodied in 'the law', justice doesn't mean anything in the real world. Hegel might argue that this concept of 'justice'/'the law' can only be grasped dialectically. Marx adopted the Hegelian dialectic as a description of the working of history, but removed from it all connotations of 'spirit', religion or what is called 'Idealism', applying it instead to strictly *materialist* or real-world criteria; hence the phrase associated with Marxism, 'dialectical materialism'. What this meant in practice was that in place of the Hegelian 'spiritual' or 'ideal' dialectic of history Marx argued for a 'real-world' narrative, in which the conflict suggested by the dialectic is acted out by humanity, with history as the conflict between different classes. As Marx and Engels put it in *The Communist Manifesto*, 'the history of all hitherto existing society is the history of class struggles.' For Marx the end result of this dialectic – the material synthesis to arise from the clash of bourgeoisie and proletariat – would be Communism. Jameson as a critic is deeply committed to dialectical approaches; his neat definition of the term is 'stereoscopic thinking' (*LM*: 28), the ability to encounter and think through both sides of any argument.

The drift of Hegelianism is towards a totality, a transcendent 'oneness'. Hegel, for instance, believed in the importance of understanding the whole enormous narrative of history, not as one period following another, but rather as a single, total thing, a *totality* expressing the working out of the dialectic of spirit. He was happier dealing with big structures than with individual particulars. He preferred, for instance, to think of 'the state' rather than individual people, and in fact refused to believe that individuals actually existed by themselves: 'only in the state does man have a rational existence,' he wrote in 1830, 'man owes his entire existence to the state, and has his being within it alone. Whatever worth and spiritual reality he possesses are his solely by virtue of the state' (Hegel: 414). Above all Hegel believed in an absolute knowledge, which he envisaged as a complete spiritual comprehension in unity; a vision of totality in which all the various component parts express the essence of that whole. This sounds a little obscure (and people are still arguing exactly what Hegel meant); the important thing for us is that many Marxist traditions have seen Marx as adopting Hegelian philosophy and then cleaning out all its mystical, spiritual and idealist elements, leaving a *materialist* philosophy of totality. Some people have seen it as a short step from this to a practical Marxism in which, like the Stalinism that dominated the Soviet Union through the 1940s and 1950s, individuals are denied rights because they are considered unimportant compared to the 'totality' of the state. In other words, it is a short step to oppressive totalitarianism. This, according to Althusser, was not only a great wrong, it was a misreading of Marx.

In his 1965 book *For Marx*, Althusser went back to Marx and argued that, although *early* Marx was influenced by Hegel, *later* Marx moved beyond Hegel and abandoned all the dangerous 'totalism' of that philosophy. Althusser argued that if you read Marx with the proper attention, you saw a 'break' in his developing career, a break between the early Hegelian Marx and the later 'scientific' one, a philosophy purged of the dangerous Hegelianism of the earlier work. Accordingly, Althusser was uncomfortable with analysing society and culture in terms of 'social orders' or 'total systems' because such usages suggest that the world is a monolithic structure with a rigid pattern and a centre that absolutely determines all the aspects of that form. Instead, Althusser uses terms such as 'social formation', stressing the ways in which society is a decentred structure – a more complex system with many elements in interrelations rather than a single rigid structure. To use a more up-to-date term, Althusser was interested in the *deconstruction* of the totality.

To take one specific example: I outlined above the Marxist notion of 'base' and 'superstructure', suggesting that a vulgar Marxist reading of that structure saw everything that happened in the superstructure (from law and religion to art and culture) as being rigidly defined by the base. Althusser radically revises this concept. So Marxists at the turn of the century saw that people behaved badly to other people, oppressing them in various ways. The reason society was so unjust, a classic Marxist might have said, was that the economic base of society was unjust. So (for instance) people competed against one another and made one another miserable, *because* the economic base of society – capitalism – was based on the principles of exploitation and violent competition for the ownership of the means of production. Many Marxists reasoned that if the *base* were changed, then the *superstructure* would follow suit and change too: that if a capitalist economy were replaced with a *socialist* economy, then people would stop competing with one another and instead start working together. This was tried in many countries, and (not to beat around the bush) it didn't work. In general it was found that if you removed money as a reason for people to compete and hurt one another, then they instead competed and hurt one another for other reasons (for instance, status or sex). If the base was changed, many features of the superstructure refused to follow suit.

Why was this? Clearly there is such a thing as 'the economy' and there are such things as 'attitudes and structures of belief'; but if the relationship between the two is not so simple as one causing the other, then what exactly *is* the relationship? Althusser argued that the relationship between base and superstructure was not simply one of cause (base) and effect (superstructure). These things were not parts of the same Hegelian organic totality, but had what he called 'relative autonomy'. In some ways the base does determine the superstructure, but in other ways the superstructure (what people think and believe) determines the base (the way the economy is structured), and in other ways the two are relatively free of one another. Althusser never denied that, as he put it, 'in the last instance' the root of society was economic, that if you followed the chain of causation far enough down you would always eventually come back to the economic realities of life. But he radically revised the way the model was conceptualised.

The question of precisely how the base determines the superstructure is vitally important to any Marxist critic because it will pinpoint exactly what sort of criticism we should undertake in order best to understand the productions of culture. A vulgar Marxist critic might content him- or herself with explaining the economic facts behind Dickens' novels or James Cameron's film *Titanic* (1998) – indeed, would see the texts are mere expressions of underlying economic and class issues: but an Althusserian insists that it is not as simple as that. The vulgar Marxist sees *Titanic* as a simple attempt to distract ordinary people from the reality of their economic positions with a love story that suggests romance conquers the class divide; or alternately they might see the film as a naked celebration of conspicuous consumption (it was the most expensive movie ever made). An Althusserian, on the other hand, would tend to be interested in the contradictions and gaps in the film, seeing it as a wide-ranging signifying structure rather than as just an element in one straightforward totality. It would be possible, in this way, to find more positive readings of the film – a film, after all, implicated in enormous capital investment, a film specifically about class differences and the mystification of romantic love. In a way, we could see *Titanic* as being about capitalist waste of money, about bourgeois decadence meeting the iron force of necessity in the shape of the iceberg.

Jameson devotes a lengthy section at the beginning of *The Political Unconscious* to elaborating Althusser's ideas and to working through this problem of what is the proper basis for interpretation. As he puts it, his own enterprise, 'the enterprise of constructing a properly Marxist hermeneutic' ('hermeneutic' means the theory and practice of interpretation) 'must necessarily confront the powerful objections to traditional models of interpretation raised by the influential school of...Althusserian Marxism' (*PU*: 23). Jameson is a little more cautious than Althusser. He does not think, for instance, that the old-fashioned straightforward causal model of base–superstructure can be entirely banished from Marxist interpretation, and he gives an example of what he sees as an instance of precisely that in recent literary history.

> There seems, for instance, to have been an unquestionable causal relationship between the admittedly extrinsic fact of the crisis in late nineteenth-century publishing, during which the dominant three-decker lending library novel was

replaced by a cheaper one-volume format, and the modification of the 'inner
form' of the novel itself.

(PU: 25)

In other words, Jameson identifies the fact that there was a change in
the dominant type of novel being written towards the end of the nineteenth-century away from the more fantastic, imaginative fictions of a
writer like Charles Dickens (1812–70) and towards the more tightly
controlled realist fiction of a novelist like George Gissing
(1857–1903). He then argues that any analysis of how and why that
change came about must take account of the economic changes in the
'base' of the publishing industry: indeed, he is saying that these
economic changes determined the shift in form of the novel, in a
straightforward 'base determines superstructure' model. But although
Jameson thinks there might be occasions when this model of causality
applies, such 'mechanical causality' is not the whole story, but is
instead only 'one of the various laws and subsystems' of our 'social and
cultural life' (*PU*: 26).

Specifically, Jameson relates almost everything he writes to a particular 'total' system, the enfolding dynamic of class and social forces over
time. He kicks off *The Political Unconscious* with a famous, unambiguous
slogan: 'always historicize!'. In this sense Jameson needs to be seen as a
'historicist' thinker.

HISTORICISM

In general terms, 'historicism' is a belief that no critical account of a text
can be complete without a sense of the historical context in which it was
produced and received. In Marxist traditions, the term has been more
carefully argued through, with particular attention being paid to what
'history' is in the first place. Marxist thinker Walter Benjamin (1882–1940)
criticised thinkers who believed history was 'in the past' – which is to say,
finished and complete – or who believed that history was a narrative of
progress culminating in the present day. For Benjamin, history is fragmented, disruptive and continually being filtered through and present in
the contemporary world. History, for Benjamin, should be understood not
as a smooth narrative moving towards a specific ending, but a discontinuous array of power struggles and exploitation. Althusser wrote an article

called 'Marxism is not an historicism' (1979) which, as its title suggests, denied that history should be a shaping force in Marxist analysis. Jameson himself has written an article called 'Marxism and historicism' (*IT2*) that focuses on the shifts of 'modes of production' – ways of producing commodities and structuring the economy – the shift, for instance, from a feudal to a capitalist mode of production. For Jameson, the present is a site contested by past and future histories, 'now' being a composite of the traces of the past and anticipations of the future present in our contemporary mode of production.

For Jameson everything must be historicised; even historicism itself. 'Always historicize!' – as an example of how self-reflexive this statement is (which is to say, the ways in which our present-day historicising needs also to be historicised), he provides a 'historical' context for Althusser's mistrust of totalising, giving a 'total' context for an anti-totalising philosophy which might be thought a little cheeky. Jameson suggests that the Althusserian distaste for 'totalization' of the Hegelian sort in fact reflects a hatred not of Hegel but Stalin (Althusser's 'Hegel' is actually 'a secret code word for Stalin' (*PU*: 37)). Jameson picks out Althusser's criticism of 'allegorical' readings of history – like Hegel's – where the various events of human history are read as all fitting together into some grand unifying or totalising pattern. A religious person, for example, might think that everything that happens in history is not important in itself, but instead as symbolical elements in 'God's plan'; a vulgar Marxist might insist that everything is part of the totality of 'class struggle' and 'dialectical materialism'. Althusser, on the contrary, insists that 'history is a process without a *telos* [end or aim] or a subject' [quoted by Jameson, *PU*: 29]. Jameson reads Althusser's attack on 'allegorical history' as also being an attack on the old version of base and superstructure.

The more general attack on allegorical master codes also implies a specific critique of the vulgar Marxist theory of levels, whose conception of base and superstructure, with the related notion of the 'ultimately determining instance' of the economic, can be shown, when diagrammed in the following way, to have some deeper kinship with the allegorical [readings of history]:

Superstructures	CULTURE IDEOLOGY (philosophy, religion, etc.) THE LEGAL SYSTEM POLITICAL SUPERSTRUCTURES AND THE STATE
Base or infrastructure	((RELATIONS OF PRODUCTION (classes) THE ECONOMIC MODE OF PRODUCTION ((FORCES OF PRODUCTION (technology, ecology, population)

(PU: 32)

Jameson insists that 'this orthodox schema is still essentially an allegorical one'. What this means for the literary or cultural critic is that he or she runs the risk of taking 'the cultural text' as 'an essentially allegorical model of society as a whole, its tokens and elements' (*PU*: 33). Althusser does not want to fit together all the disparate elements into a single signifying totality, but he does want to hold them in the same argument and say worthwhile things about them. His preferred metaphor for doing this is not assembling a 'structure' with its (for him) bad connotations of centre and totality, but instead a *Darstellung*, the German word for 'representation'. Jameson gives us a different model from the 'vulgar Marxist' one reproduced above to 'convey the originality' of Althusser's conception.

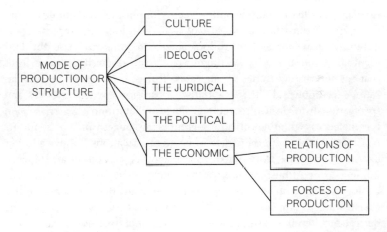

(PU: 36)

This model is much less formally structured than the previous one of 'base' and 'superstructure'. It branches in various directions, and it shows how aspects of society like 'Culture' or 'Law' are not directly determined by the economy, but are instead 'semi-autonomous' (*PU*: 37), linked only through a common logic of organisation or structure. This may all seem rather dryly technical, of interest chiefly to theoretical Marxists; but Jameson is adamant that 'this conception of structure should make it possible to understand the otherwise incomprehensible prestige and influence of the Althusserian revolution – which has produced powerful and challenging oppositional currents in a host of disciplines, from philosophy proper to political science, anthropology, legal studies, economics, and cultural studies.' (*PU*: 37). An Althusserian critic is never going to be seduced by the gesture towards the sweeping generalisation, but will always pay attention to the particulars of any given text without, of course, losing sight of the fact that there are larger systems that apply (capitalism, for instance). For example, an older Marxist critic such as Theodor Adorno dismissed Hollywood films as instances (in the superstructure) of the repressive economic conditions of capitalist America (the base): it didn't matter which film we might cite, as far as Adorno was concerned they were all part of a malign 'culture industry' designed to fool the masses with empty dreams into ignoring the misery of their circumstances. Adorno has been very influential, not least on Jameson, but a post-Althusserian critic would not want to subscribe to any such reductive totalising judgement. Clearly, Hollywood is deeply implicated in capitalism, and many of the films that come out of it are ideologically unpleasant or dubious. But we might want to look at specific films and tease out their ideological significances; we might want to distinguish between films that say interesting things about capitalism (the powerful and exhilarating critique of the capitalist obsession with 'work' and 'professionalism' in a film such as Quentin Tarantino's *Reservoir Dogs*, for instance) without entirely surrendering our suspicion about its place, as a product, in the world of economic relations. To give another example, this time from Slavoj Zizek, another contemporary Marxist influenced by Althusser. He says that living as we are 'in the midst of ecological catastrophe' it is 'especially important that we conceive this catastrophe as...meaningless'. That may seem like a rather strange desire, but it reflects what he sees as an imperative not to surrender interpretation to any pseudo-totality: 'i.e. that we do not "read meanings into things," as is done by those who interpret the ecological crisis as a "deeper sign" of punishment for our merciless exploitation of nature, etc.' (Zizek: 140). To do that would be to get in the way of a proper understanding of the phenomena that make up the contemporary ecological situation, to be distracted by a imaginary 'ideal' unity where there isn't one.

Jameson's breadth of subject, so that as we noted at the beginning of the Why Jameson? section 'nothing cultural is alien to him', is in this sense much more Althusserian than Hegelian. He sees many texts as interesting and useful that a vulgar Marxist would simply dismiss as 'false consciousness', and he is thoroughly suspicious of over-generalised or sweeping critical judgements.

One final point that is worth making about Althusser is the extent to which his particular animus against 'oppressive totalities', and his insistence of decentring, parallels the developments in literary criticism and philosophy that are now identified under the umbrella title of 'deconstruction'. For the moment it is merely worth noting that the parallels with what Jameson (in 1981) called 'the current post-structural celebration of discontinuity and heterogeneity' are not precise; that for Althusser this deconstructive strategy 'is only an initial movement in Althusserian exegesis, which then requires the fragments, the incommensurable levels, the heterogeneous impulses, of the text to be once again related, but in the mode of structural difference and determinate contradiction' (*PU*: 56). To put it crudely, the various social and cultural determinants of art do need to be 'deconstructed', but an Althusserian Marxist also needs to reconstruct, even if that reconstruction remains aware of the contradictions it contains, because any Marxist needs to be able to make a certain, political sense of what he or she is doing. There are constants in human history (mostly constants, it has to be said, of oppression and human misery); and however important it is to interpret and to establish the grounds for interpretation, there is a more fundamental Marxist injunction: not just to interpret the world, but to change it.

SUMMARY

There are a number of concepts and ideas derived from Marx that are essential basics for any reader of Jameson, and these include:

- The *materialism* of the approach.
- The concept of *ideology*.
- The process of the *dialectic*.
- The complex relations between economic *base* and ideological *superstructure*.

2

JAMESON'S MARXISMS

Marxism and Form and *Late Marxism*

The previous chapter sketched out the Marxist contexts from which Jameson's own writings have emerged. But, as has been noted, Jameson's engagements with Marxism are more complex than can be simply represented in a general introduction to 'Marxism'. Nor do the conventional accounts of Jameson's Marxism usually do him justice. That is to say, it is not enough to put Jameson in a box marked 'Hegelian Marxist' and oppose him to the more post-structuralist Marxisms that can be broadly characterised as 'Althusserian'. America is a country without the prominent tradition of social democratic or labour parties of many European cultures. At times in its history, particularly when Jameson was a young man, the USA has been extremely hostile to 'Marxism', and this has given Jameson a slightly different perspective on Marx than might have been the case with a critic growing up in a European country for which 'socialism' has been less marginal. Quite apart from anything else, it gave Jameson a repu-tation as the first to introduce American readers to the work of such powerful Marxist theorists as Georg Lukacs and Theodor Adorno.

Terry Eagleton has argued that, out of the full panoply of concepts available to the Marxist thinker, Jameson has been fascinated chiefly with just two: reification and commodification. 'His ruling political concepts,' Eagleton suggests, 'inherited from Lukacs and [Adorno], are those of reification and commodification. The power and versatility of insight that Jameson can generate from those twin notions is little short of staggering.' (Eagleton 1986: 63). This is a bit of a caricature, but it is true that Jameson's own Marxism has been most powerfully influenced by Lukacs and Adorno, and that concepts derived from these thinkers are central to his own writings. This chapter looks at what these ideas are: Lukacs' 'reification', the Adorno version of 'the dialectic' and his suspicion of 'commodification', and the whole 'Hegelian' fascination with totality. It concentrates chiefly on *Marxism and Form* (1971), an early book that widely established Jameson as America's foremost Marxist critic, and on *Late Marxism* (1990), his lesser-known study of Adorno, touching also on a few other essays.

MARXISM AND TOTALITY

It is worth going back over some of the points raised in the previous chapter about Marxism. Althusser's perspective, that a Marxist concentration on 'totality' slides too easily into 'totalitarian' politics and needs to be resisted, leaves little room for a thinker in the more Hegelian traditions. Why do some of these thinkers, including Jameson, think that 'total vision' is not only desirable, but essential to any Marxist perspective?

For many it is precisely the totalising or systematising cast of Marxism that makes it attractive, and makes it such a penetrating tool for analysing the world around us. We might introduce an example, here, which could be something as simple as a man in Washington DC buying a hot dog for his lunch. The man is dressed in an expensive designer suit and speaking on his mobile phone; he is white, well-educated, working in government, and in a hurry. The man serving him the hot dog works as a fast-food vendor on the street; he is black, poorly-educated, lives in government-subsidised accommodation and has the sense that his life is going nowhere and can go nowhere. Let's assume that both of these men have IQs of 150. This is a particular scenario, not a general one (some of the people who work selling hot dogs in the USA are white; some of the customers are black, of course), but if we wanted to understand why this one man has money, status and power and the other doesn't we could approach the question in a number of ways. If we believed in a 'free market' or 'capitalist' philosophy we could argue that the man with the mobile phone has worked harder, pushed himself further, applied himself more, and has realised the American dream; where the other man has failed to motivate himself or 'make something of his life'. From this point of view, it is simply a matter of two individuals; the fact that one grew up in a poor black ghetto and the other in an affluent middle-class suburb is merely circumstantial. A Labour Party or Democratic Party approach to the same scenario might see that issues of the class in which you are born, the facts of racism and the limitations on opportunity play a part, but that the overall system, capitalism, nonetheless provided adequate opportunity for self-realisation and does not need changing. Again, for this system of beliefs, the issue can be tackled individually by, for instance, providing more scholarship or government-subsidised opportunities for poor people to access education and so better themselves. But many Marxists, to instance a third choice, would be liable to say that this situation cannot be understood in isolation. In order to comprehend it is necessary to think it through *systematically* to see how the totality of society and culture manifests itself in this particular instance. So, it is not enough to say that this particular man is black; we need to understand that black people in America, as a whole, tend to be poorer, die younger, have lower-paid and lower-status jobs, and so on, and that this individual is one example of the total picture. We need to examine the way the system as a whole concentrates wealth with a small minority and excludes the majority; to look at, for instance, the fact that Washington, the seat of government, has an overwhelmingly black population whilst only a small proportion of officials in higher government are black.

In turn this needs to be put in a totalising *historical* perspective: to see, for instance, that the history of slavery and the subsequent history of segregation and racism in America have created social and cultural structures that disadvantage black people. The focus here is on race, whereas most Marxists are more comfortable talking about class (so they might argue that the fact that this man is black is not as important as the fact that he is poor), but the strength of this sort of approach is that it refuses to be distracted by individual counter-examples, the exceptions to the rule. Will Smith is wealthy; he might be instanced as 'proof' that America is not racially biased, proof that it is possible for a black man to succeed. But this is the particular; the total portrait is that *most* black men and women in America are poorer than most white people. The result of this, which is enormous human misery and oppression, needs to be kept in sight. Any of the key problems facing

the world today (starvation and disease in the developing world; envi-
ronmental crisis; warfare; violence) can only be understood by seeing
them not as isolated issues but as part of a global, total system. They
can (say the Marxists) be cured, but only if the problems are addressed
properly.

CULTURE AND IDEOLOGY

Literary and cultural studies are, from a Marxist perspective, implicated in the whole system of society too, and critics need to
understand them as such. This is less obvious than the example of the
hot-dog vendor, partly because many artists have seen art as a special
arena, separated from the hurly-burly of politics and society. How can
it be said that a painting by Leonardo da Vinci (1452–1519), a piano
sonata by Beethoven (1770–1827), or a poem by Wallace Stevens
(1878–1955) are 'political'? More particularly, a woman standing rapt
in front of the *Mona Lisa*, or listening with eyes closed to the triplets of
the *Moonlight Sonata*, may feel that the art is actually transporting her
away from the grubbiness of her real life. Many Marxists would
counter this by pointing out that each of these artefacts was produced,
like a chair or a car, for money or out of a circumstance in which the
artists financial needs were taken care of so that he could produce; that
art is bought and sold just like chairs and cars; that art makes money
for some people and not others, often making more money for people
who possess capital than it ever did for the artist who produced it; so
that the illusion of distance from 'the economic' is just that, an illusion.
Moreover, it may be that it is precisely this illusion that is the point of
the art. Theodor Adorno, for instance, considered any art that provided
compensatory pleasures of escapism from the brutalities of modern
living was a dangerous lie and needed to be challenged, although I
should add that he would not have put Beethoven or Stevens into that
category. There is a more crucial way, however, in which the painting,
piano piece or poem needs to be thought of as 'political' in the broad
sense – the broad sense being not so much to do with how you vote in
the next election, as with how society as a whole is structured and
your place in it. That sense is *ideological*. As mentioned earlier, Jameson
follows Althusser in seeing ideology not just as 'false-consciousness',
but as the structures of thought and feeling that define us as citizens in
late capitalist society. Culture has a large part to play in this form of

ideology – an increasing part, eclipsing now the roles played by education, religion and patriotism. We learn much of how to act, what to believe, how to perform and indeed how to *be* from the culture around us. Take another example. A young man is dressed in fashionably baggy clothes and listening to music through his walkman. He says: 'I love music, my life is music, and I simply don't care about politics.'

The mistake here is in thinking that something like 'music' can be usefully separated out from politics and society in general. Saying 'I just want to dance' is, on one level, just saying that, but pretending that it goes no further than you having a good time is merely to be blind to the ways in which your dancing, leisure culture, the music industry and culture at large exploit, condition and ideologise. This person may think, may even really believe, that he can 'magically' separate himself out from politics and economics; but the reality is that his chosen art is deeply implicated in precisely these things: the music industry *is* an industry. From an Adorno-esque perspective, it might be thought to be an industry that serves the interests of capitalism extremely well, not merely by making so much money, but by distracting people, convincing them to put their energies into dancing all night or taking drugs, rather than getting interested in trying to change the manifest injustices in our world.

Terry Eagleton has another example of what I am talking about here, not relating to culture. He considers the sentence 'Prince Charles is a thoughtful, conscientious fellow', arguing that this 'may be true as far as it goes' but it erroneously 'isolates the object known as Prince Charles from the whole context of the institution of royalty'. Concentrating on the individual personality of Prince Charles is to miss the point; only by understanding the situation and history of royalty in Britain, its wealth and continuing power and influence and the ways in which many Britons subscribe to an ideology that reinforces these inequalities, can Prince Charles' true position be understood. In other words, Eagleton follows Hegel in arguing that 'it is only by the operation of dialectical reason that such static, discrete phenomena can be reconstituted as a dynamic, developing whole' (Eagleton 1991: 98–9). These are views, then, rather differently weighted to the Althusserian anti-Hegelianism I mentioned in Chapter 1. Althusser would have agreed with them insofar as he believed that life was still determined by the economic *in the last instance*, so that the economic provides a sort of back-drop 'totality' against which our analysis always takes place, but he would have found the principle of always looking for the total system rather than the individual too close to Stalinist totalitarianism for comfort. More recent deconstruction-influenced Marxists have doubted that there even *is* a coherent 'totality' to apprehend.

A representation of this might be found in the recent SF blockbuster film *The Matrix* (1999), surely one of the most Marxist films ever to come out of Hollywood. In that film, a character called 'Neo' (Keanu Reeves) discovers that the life he thought he was living in 1990 America is actually an elaborate computer-generated virtual reality (the 'Matrix' of the title), designed by evil machine intelligences to hide from people the truth that their existence has been reduced to lying helpless in mechanised pods whilst machines siphon off the biological electricity and energy their bodies produce. The Matrix exists, Neo is told, to obscure the truth – 'the truth that you are a slave'. Neo is disabused of the false appearance of his reality, and wakes up in the distinctly unpleasant pod, in order to join a resistance move-ment fighting this evil. In other words, if we ask what the 'Matrix' is, then the answer is that it *is* ideology in the Marxist sense of a fiction obscuring the truth of exploitation. In fact, this film articulates a more thorough-going Althusserian or Jamesonian sense of what ideology is: 'the Matrix' is more than a set of false beliefs about reality (or false consciousness) – it *is* reality, it conditions and defines how the people caught up in themselves think and act. In the world of *The Matrix* it would do no good to address this piecemeal issue or that one; the only answer is the total vision, a full comprehension of how the entire system works to blot out the consciousness of oppression.

REIFICATION

Georg Lukacs (1885–1971) joined the Hungarian Communist Party in his twenties, and was thoroughly committed to a 'Hegelian' whole vision of social wrongs. An early work, regarded by some as his most significant work, was *History and Class Consciousness* (1923), which is based on a totalising vision of society and history, and diagnoses the ills of society as deriving from *alienation* and *reification*, concepts Lukacs derived and elaborated from Marx. 'Alienation' is discussed in Chapter 1, but 'reification' is a crucial concept for Lukacs, and through him for Jameson.

REIFICATION

The word means 'the transformation of a person, process or abstract concept into a thing', and this 'thingification' was part of Marx's diagnoses of the ills of society. Marx noted the ways in which, under capitalism, human powers and creativities seemed to escape human control and take on lives of their own: so, for instance, 'market forces' are often invoked today as if they were a force of nature like gravity instead of the product of human interaction. These estranged or alienated forces can come to dominate and oppress human existence, just as things themselves – commodities and objects – become treated as if they were important, or even more important than people. For Lukacs, reification becomes an even more important concept. It is seen as being the root of many, if not most, of the problems of contemporary society. It operates in two ways. One is the way in which capitalism defines everything in commodity terms because everything has an 'exchange value', an amount of money for which it can be bought and sold. This rates one 'thing' – money – as more important than any other thing (for instance, human beings and the quality of their existence); in Jameson's words, it involves 'the substitution for human relations of thing-like ones' such as money (*LM*: 180). In addition to this, reification sees the triumph of the commodity, and the subsequent eclipse of the sense of society as an organic whole. In place of seeing the whole picture, people see now only the things, the commodities, provided by capitalism; people desire not social harmony and justice but rather a wide-screen TV or a DVD player. The 'wholeness' of social life is shattered into sporadic dispersions of specialised, machine-like or technical objects and operations, each of which has the potential to assume a near-life of its own and dominate actual human beings. Several Marxist theorists have analysed this 'reified' fragmentation of contemporary life, which they see as the direct result of capitalism. Jameson talks about Walter Benjamin's 'straining towards a psychic wholeness' amongst 'a vision of a world in ruins and fragments' (*M&F*: 61), or about Sartre's critique of 'our fragmented and atomistic society' in which 'matter has been invested with human energy and henceforth takes the place of and functions like human action. The machine is of course the most basic symbol of this type of structure' (*M&F*: 244).

There is much about Lukacs' writing that seems a little crude or (to some people) misguided today. For example, Jameson is dismissive of Lukacs belief in a 'reflection' theory of art, which is to say that art simply 'reflects' the reality around it; and, it is true, there are few critics working today who would be comfortable with this sort of theory. More than this, Jameson thinks that Lukacs had 'too incomplete and intermittent a sense of the relationship of class ideology'. But Jameson nonetheless insists that 'wrong as he might have been in the 1930s', by a strange twist, Lukacs *does* have 'some provisional last word for us today'. And it is the two categories of reification and totality that are most powerfully relevant.

> Unlike the more familiar concept of alienation…reification is a process that affects our cognitive relationship with the social totality. It is a disease of that mapping function whereby the individual subject projects and models his or her insertion into the collectivity. The reification of late capitalism – the transformation of human relations into an appearance of relationship between things – renders society opaque: it is the loved source of the mystifications on which ideology is based and by which domination and exploitation are legitimized.
>
> (*IT2*: 146)

In other words, Jameson thinks that reification is even more important to an understanding of the world today than it was when Lukacs formulated it in the 1930s because he considers the triumph of global late capitalism – the failure of Communism and the spread of capitalism all over the world – to have involved a more comprehensive *commodification* than ever before. This turning of everything into a commodity, which is something particularly evident in the worlds of art and culture, is precisely reification, the thingifying of all human creative and relational abilities. It is not just that art gets reified: that a piece of music is turned into millions of CDs, that a film is petrified as merchandising, videos and other paraphernalia, and so on. It is that actual human interaction is metamorphosed into commodities: that society moves towards the position that, for example, the only way one human being can express love for another human being is by entering into the whole world of commodities, by buying things from small gifts all the way up to houses (so that purchasing a house is seen as a 'sign of commitment' rather than what it actually is, the reification of the love itself). Under this logic things are the focus of our attention; we look at society and we can only see things, or only see the medium of things, which is to say, money.

Reification undermines the sense of totality in society, according to Jameson; it fragments our perception of the whole world in which we live, so that we can only see the frozen discrete objects that make up our existence. Our world shrinks to just those reified things – maybe music CDs, maybe cars, maybe clothes – that define our world, and we actually do begin to think things like 'all I care about is my music, politics doesn't interest me'. We become blind to the fact that we live in a total network of relationships with other people; we can only see our CDs or videos (or whatever the key commodity is for us). In this circumstance, Jameson thinks that 'art' has an important role to play. It is vital that art is able 'to resist the power of reification in consumer society and to reinvent that category of totality which [is] systematically undermined by existential fragmentation on all levels of life and social organisation today' (*IT2*: 146).

ART AND RESISTANCE

How can 'art' do this? The answer, suggests Jameson, is perhaps not as obvious as it might seem. The important strategy is that of resistance, and this is something that Jameson takes most fully from Adorno. For Adorno, culture had been poisoned by capitalism and turned into 'the Culture Industry', an all-embracing capitalist commodification of art that reduced everything to the level of a Hollywood B-movie or a pop-song. A book Adorno wrote with a colleague, Max Horkheimer, called *The Dialectic of Enlightenment* (1944) contains a powerfully argued chapter on 'The Culture Industry' that attacks popular American culture of the 1930s and 1940s as designedly dull and repetitive, feeding the populace minimal variations of the same oppressive stories of love and adventure in order to stupefy them, to turn them into sheep and so effectively to defuse their revolutionary potential. Adorno is particularly famous as a critic of music and his attacks on 'Jazz' and early pop are particularly sharp: he saw Jazz as standardised music, in something like the same way that hamburger joints deliver standardised food and factories deal in standardised parts. A pop song shuffles a few limited components around, and teaches its fans that pleasure lies in recognising the familiar and acquiescing, rather than in resistance and the encounter with novelty. In the final analysis, Adorno saw this as a straightforward tool of social oppression: the dull repetitive music and dull repetitive films conditioning people into accepting their dull repetitive jobs and lives, into thinking that this dullness and repetition is somehow natural instead of a symptom of capitalist oppression. Against the evils of popular culture (as he saw them) Adorno championed art that was difficult, that challenged and resisted easy enjoyment, precisely because this art was liable to shake up our expectations and prevent us from simply going along with what we are given. So, whilst he hated 'jazz' and popular music, he wrote sensitively about the experimental atonal music of Arnold Schoenberg (1874–1951). By inventing a new musical scale, the twelve-tone system, Schoenberg broke from the music that had been composed in the more conventional musical major and minor scales. Many people find his music discordant and even unpleasant to listen to, but for Adorno that is the point; Schoenberg compels listeners to attend to the fact that *they are listening*. As Jameson puts it, with conventional music such as film scores or pop songs people no longer actually hear the notes of the music; rather the music is merely felt 'as a signal for the release of the appropriate conventionalized reaction. The musical composition becomes mere psychological stimulus or conditioning, as in those airports or supermarkets where the customer is aurally tranquilized.' Accordingly there is some point in the 'ugliness' of a composer like Schoenberg, as if 'only the painful remained as a spur to perception' (*M&F*: 23–4).

Jameson goes on to point out that what holds true for music holds true for language as well. Adorno saw the greatest opportunities for resisting the system not in works of realism (as Lukacs did), where, as in a novel like Emile Zola's *Germinal* (1885) the evils of society can be laid before the reader directly. Instead Adorno's judgement (Jameson elsewhere calls it 'rather astonishing', *IT2*: 143) is that it is Samuel Beckett who is the most revolutionary of writers because, like Schoenberg, Beckett remade language as something difficult, something in a sense atonal. We might also think of various 'difficult' experimental stylists and poets. Perhaps contemporary poetry has a reputation for obscurity, but 'it is enough' says Jameson

to evoke the fad for rapid reading and the habitual conscious or unconscious skimming of newspaper and advertising slogans, for us to understand the deeper social reasons for the stubborn insistence of modern poetry on the materiality and density of language, on words felt not as transparency but rather as things in themselves. So also in the realm of philosophy the bristling jargon of seemingly private languages is to be evaluated against the advertising copybook recommendations of 'clarity' as the essence of 'good writing'; whereas the latter seeks to hurry the reader past his own received ideas, difficulty is inscribed in the former as the sign of the effort which must be made to think real thoughts.

(*M&F*: 24)

With this we come back to a point raised in the first section. This argument also works as a justification for Jameson's own 'difficult' writing style.

FORM VERSUS CONTENT

One crucial aspect of this is that the emphasis is on *form* rather than *content*. To return to the contrast suggested above. Zola's *Germinal* is a novel written in a lucid, clear style, describing with documentary verisimilitude the dreadful conditions of working miners in nineteenth-century France. It is a powerful and moving book that engages the reader in the sufferings of its ordinary protagonists. Samuel Beckett's novels, on the other hand, are 'about' very little: a bedridden man contemplating his life as he dies; a tramp wandering about Paris and ending up sleeping in an unused carriage. But his language is deliberately clotted, broken; his use of form is fractured and innovative; he can be difficult to read. It might seem common-sense to say that Zola is the more useful writer in a Marxist sense, but Jameson spends the whole of *Marxism and Form* exploring the possibility that the truth is actually the other way around. In this he is following Adorno, who believed that it was the *form* of a work of art – its genre, structure, style – that was the most important thing, and its *content* – story, character, setting – was only secondary. It is not that content is unimportant, but it is the formal aspect of art that has the greatest revolutionary potential, and it is innovations in the form such as Schoenberg's twelve-tone scale or Beckett's distinctive prose that represents the most progressive aspects of contemporary art.

Adorno's ultimate philosophical position seems to me to be...[that] the content of a work of art stands judged by its form, and that it is the realized form of the

work that offers the surest key to the vital possibilities of that determinate
social moment from which it springs.

(*M&F*: 55)

This is quite a startling position, but it is one that Jameson argues
coherently not merely through *Marxism and Form*, but also through
many of his other, later books. Most famously this is the burden of *The
Political Unconscious* – that the key ideological aspect of nineteenth-
century literature is its particular *form* of narrative, not its supposed
content.

One consequence of this approach is that it allows the critic to
analyse literature with an illuminating emphasis on the formal. So,
given that Lukacs yearned for a total vision, for the ability to see the
whole picture rather than just fragmented pieces of it, he was drawn to
the reading of Homeric epic. In his early study *The Theory of the Novel*
(1916) he praised the coherent vision of Greek epic, in which the very
form of the epic poem embodies the organic totality of Greek culture.
He contrasted this with the nineteenth-century novel, which could not
embody such a totality because the society out of which it grew was
radically fragmented and broken, by the reification of capitalism. That
the novel embodies a fragmented aesthetic was, for Lukacs, again a
formal issue, which had to do with (for instance) the gap between the
position of narrator and that of hero in nineteenth-century fiction.
Another manifestation of this is the way the nineteenth-century historical novel represents great men from history (as it might be Napoleon
or Cromwell) in passing, as characters that the ordinary workaday hero
encounters by-the-way. This contrasts with, say, Shakespeare (or more
modern dramatists) who put their historically famous individuals
squarely at the centre of their plays. As Jameson puts it:

> The great historical figures, the real leading actors in history, will be central in
> drama (Macbeth, Wallenstein, Galileo) because the dramatic collision is a far
> more concentrated and heightened one; whereas the novel, which aims at a
> total picture of the historical background, can only tolerate such figures in
> secondary, episodic appearances, for it is only in such a distant, secondary way
> that they appear in our everyday lives, in our own lived experience.

(*M&F*: 194)

We are back, in a way, at base and superstructure; a fragmented, reified society produces fragmented, reified art – this, at least, is how Lukacs saw it. The novel is the dominant form of literature in the nineteenth century precisely because it embodies – formally – the qualities of fragmented sprawl, of ironic disintegration of vision and reified existence that are present in nineteenth-century lived experience. This feature of the novel as a mode is more important than the content of these novels, which is often conventional and escapist, with an emphasis on happy marriages and plot resolutions tying up all the loose ends. In later books, Jameson will argue (see Chapter 6) that cinema and TV are the dominant forms of art today because it is in these visual media that the conditions of postmodern society are most thoroughly expressed.

THE PERSISTENCE OF THE DIALECTIC

Reification, then, involves the fragmentation and destruction of the totality of existence; and it must be resisted. Art and literature are vital to a Marxist because they can (although not in all cases) provide means of refreshing our sense of this totality, and perhaps more importantly can actively resist the fragmentation of existence. This 'resistance' is something Jameson is drawn to at a deep level, but it is not a matter of blindly saying 'no' to everything. One of the central insights of Adorno's thought, one that Jameson elaborates at length in *Late Marxism*, is that it is a dialectical process. As he puts it in his chapter on Adorno in *Marxism and Form*, this is what the 'dialectic' is: 'The dialectical method is precisely this preference for the concrete totality over the separate, abstract parts' (*M&F*: 45).

We saw earlier what 'the dialectic' has been to the Marxist traditions that have used the term. For Jameson, the term has a wider and more supple sense of applications. Partly this is because 'dialectics' are a *metacritical* mode of thinking, a way of doing criticism that always keeps it aware of itself: 'dialectical thinking is a thought to the second power, a thought about thinking itself, in which the mind must deal with its own thought process just as much as with the material it works on' (*M&F*: 45). But more than this, the dialectical method provides a way out of the reified desert of contemporary life.

Adorno, as Jameson argues in *Late Marxism*, looked with horror on what capitalism had done to human existence, although in place of the term 'reification' he tended to use the terms 'standardization' and 'identity'. 'Identity' for Adorno means 'things being identical with one another', and is the circumstance of capitalism where a single faceless thing – for instance, money – supersedes all the variety and difference of humanity. As Jameson puts it, Adorno sets himself against identity and 'the face it wears and turns on daily life – namely, repetition as such, the return of sameness over and over again, in all its psychological desolation and tedium' (*LM*: 16). Art can resist this tedium, but for Adorno popular culture is complicit with it: pop songs, films, popular novels and the like are all repetitive, expressions of sameness. As Adorno argued in his challenging philosophical work *Negative Dialectics* (1966), this identity permeated society and culture from top to bottom: which means that resistance to sameness cannot be piecemeal, but has to involve a systematic and dialectical refusal to be a willing part of the commodified capitalist system, a sustained negativity that revised what 'dialectics' were usually thought of as being. 'Negative Dialectics', the phrase he coined for this mode of sustained thought, does, he conceded, 'flout tradition.' 'As early as Plato,' Adorno argues, 'dialectics meant to achieve something positive by means of negation'. Adorno's own work, however, distrusts this 'positiveness' because it is insufficiently rigorous in its capacity to attack the capitalist 'identity', its crushing sameness. 'This book seeks to free dialectics from such affirmative traits without reducing its determinacy…dialectics is the consistent sense of nonidentity' (Adorno xix: 5). Jameson notes this way of avoiding being 'lock[ed] into sameness', of finding 'a mode of access to difference and the new'. He quotes Adorno: 'Thought need not rest content in its logical regularity; it is capable of thinking against itself, without abolishing itself altogether; indeed, were definitions of the dialectic possible, that one might be worth proposing' (*LM*: 17).

In a literary critical context this starts to resemble the mode of critical thought known as deconstruction, particularly in the way it mistrusts its own premises, challenges its own bases of thought. But part of Jameson's project in *Late Marxism* is sharply to differentiate a properly conceived Marxist dialectic from deconstructionist criticism. He concedes that some may see a 'family likeness' between Adorno and 'Derrida and deconstruction', but insists that 'no very solid foundation for a 'dialogue' between [deconstruction] and Marxism will be laid by wishing away the basic differences' (*LM*: 9). Adorno is still Marxist, even if his vision of the world seems austere and even gloomy compared with the varied, complex delights of Jameson's own. For Adorno, identity is hellish and reason is an ideological tool of oppression. Jameson writes:

> 'Society precedes the subject'; thought's categories are collective and social; identity is not an option but a doom; reason and its categories are at one with the rise of civilization or capitalism, and can scarcely be transformed until the latter is transformed. But [German liberal critic] Habermas is wrong to conclude that Adorno's implacable critique of reason...paints him into the corner of irrationalism and leaves him no implicit recourse but the now familiar poststructural one of *acephale* [beheading]. He thinks so only because he cannot himself allow for the possibility or the reality of some new, genuinely dialectical thinking.
>
> (*LM*: 24)

This sort of dialectic works against systems, and with an awareness of the materiality at stake. It allows us to think things that the oppressive 'Identity' of capitalist living prevent us from thinking, to think (in Jameson's figure) 'another side' to any question, 'an external face of the concept which, like that of the moon, can never be directly visible or accessible to us' (*LM*: 25). This 'dark side of the moon' reminds Jameson of 'the notion of the "Unconscious"', and this in turn invokes the psychoanalytical theories of Freud. The next chapter is given over to sketching in the importance of Freud and Freudian thinkers to Jameson's own Marxist philosophy. But before we turn to that I want to conclude with a little further discussion of the 'bases' of Jameson's own dialectical interpretations: his belief that interpretation, the business of the critic, needs to be founded in an awareness of *history*.

INTERPRETATION AND HISTORY

According to Satya Mohanty, 'all [of] Jameson's work' is concerned with 'two key questions central to contemporary theory' (Mohanty 1997: 97). The first of these questions is: what are the bases and validity of *interpretation*, and in particular, how do the metaphors used by interpreters – critics, say – shape the interpretations they undertake? The second question has to do with *history*, and the ways history is represented. It doesn't take much to see that these are likely to be central issues for any who call themselves Marxists. Interpretation, for instance, is something that happens in many forms, from reading a book and interpreting what it is about to 'reading' the world around us. Any Marxist is going to insist that the world we live in is not simply *there*, that it is not a mere accumulation of facts, but is instead interpreted. You might think of your country as a glorious and heroic embodiment of valour and honour, or you might think of your country as an oppressive regime where the rich get richer and the poor get poorer. Either way you are *interpreting* the world around you. This process of interpretation is deeply involved in the dominant ideology of the society in which you exist, so anyone interested in forms of interpretation is going to need to be open to theories of the way ideology works. One of the roles of any Marxist critic is to open people to the possibility that their interpretation can be questioned. Maybe the royal family is not ordained by God to rule the country. Maybe Shakespeare's plays are not a patriotic celebration of God and nation, but instead a powerfully complex exploration of how power and conflict shape human affairs. This is 'hermeneutics' – the technical name for the process of interpreting texts and situations. How a critic decides between differing interpretations, and according to what basis he or she grounds those interpretations, are questions that need to be answered before any actual critical interpretation can be hazarded.

Some of Jameson's most significant contributions to criticism have to do with 'hermeneutics'. As a critic he is in the business of exploring how interpretation happens, the forces that shape it, the way it functions and is received. This is what Mohanty calls 'the metacritical question of the politics of interpretation' (Mohanty 1997: 95). It is 'metacritical' because it is a form of criticism about criticism, which is to say it looks critically at the way interpretation, or 'criticism', happens. And it is about the *politics* of interpretation because, as far as Jameson is concerned, all interpretation is political, it is all shaped by the way people relate to people and by the socio-economic realities that underlie and determine how those relationships happen.

It should be clear that this issue of the politics of interpretation is closely related to an understanding of history. For one thing, the history of a thing powerfully shapes the way it is interpreted. If you are very much in favour of the royal family, you may well believe that the present queen is the successor to an unbroken line of monarchs stretching back over a thousand years, that the weight and magnificence of that history are another justification for the wealth and power the present monarch possesses. If you are opposed to royalty you might believe the opposite, that the royal family are merely the descendants of a ruthless clan of tyrants who seized power and stole a great deal of wealth, and who have subsequently obscured their crime under the mystifying notions of divine right and the fact that it happened hundreds of years ago. Either way the *history* of royalty is crucial. To take the more literary example of Shakespeare: the way interpreters of Shakespeare come to terms with the place of history in his plays (both the way the passage of history is represented in his plays and the fact that he wrote in the sixteenth and seventeenth centuries) has political implications. To suggest, for instance, that Shakespeare is untainted by history, that he was 'not of an age but for all time', to quote Ben Jonson's famous eulogy, draws on a particular ideology. The Shakespeare who deals in 'universal verities' is one who ignores the particulars of the actual. For instance: one of the running jokes of the film *Shakespeare in Love* (1998) was that sixteenth-century London was basically the same as London in the 1990s: the same cabbies, the same literary types hanging out in bars and so on. This might be funny (indeed, many people thought it was), but we need to be aware of the implied version of history it contains, which is to say a history that doesn't change, in which things basically stay the same. The political implications of this conservatism are retrograde, because if nothing changes then there's no point in trying to change anything (poverty, say, or injustice). Of course, *Shakespeare in Love* was not explicitly saying 'don't try to change anything, don't address issues of political injustice, don't rock the boat'. But it could be argued that that was the political subtext, the implication of its version of history.

Of course, all these approaches to the issue of 'history' in Shakespeare are still interpretations, reactive and partial. A more polit- ically radical critic might argue that Shakespeare is *not* 'universal', but the product of a very particular set of cultural and political forces at the end of the sixteenth century. Shakespeare's history plays chronicle the vicissitudes of several hundred years of English history, and it would be easy to construct an argument that saw those plays, with their seemingly endless succession of kings and nobles fighting bloodily amongst themselves and dying violently, as a critique of the political power of the day. The impression of constant political flux, of history as one long and bloody war, has much more radical political implications. But this is not to say that *this* interpretation is 'right' and the previous one 'wrong'. None of us have a special access to a godlike 'truth'. Any critic – including Jameson, and you, and me – has been shaped by the particular cultural and political forces of his or her environment, and these give him or her a set of preconceptions, of ways of approaching questions that inflects the issue in certain ways. We can't help this, and none of us are 'pure' or free of these constraints. At the same time, we want to be able to claim that our interpretations are better grounded than opposing interpretations. But if all interpretation is relative, how can we say one interpretation is better than another? What benchmark can we use when comparing differing interpretations – for instance, differing critical readings of a particular text?

A deconstructivist answer to this question would be that there *is* no benchmark, no 'absolute truth' against which other statements can be judged. A Marxist, on the other hand, is liable to believe that there *is* some sort of benchmark. Marx himself, as we have seen, thought that everything in the end came down to economics. Georg Lukacs, working in the Marxist tradition, was more specific and said that interpretation was grounded ultimately in 'the industrial proletariat' – which is to say, the working classes in the industrialised nations, from whom (Marx had said) communist revolution was going to come. Some deconstructivists, amongst others, are hostile to Marxist theory for this reason; it does not surprise us (for instance) that when the deconstructivist Geoffrey Bennington reviews Jameson's *The Political Unconscious* his opposition to Jameson's project runs deep.

Nonetheless, Jameson's answer to this question of interpretation is not as straightforward as this sort of 'vulgar Marxism' of Marx or Lukacs. Jameson is not altogether hostile to the persuasiveness of much deconstructionist thought, but nonetheless he does believe there is something in which interpretation can be – in fact, has to be – grounded. To put it in bald terms, Jameson grounds his interpretation in *history*: it is history that provides the basis of judging competing interpretations. 'History' is not 'real' in the way that 'the industrial proletariat' is a group of real people in the real world; but it is nonetheless (and with some smart intellectual manoeuvring by Jameson, which is detailed later in Chapter 4) a sort of absolute. It is less an absolute benchmark, more a 'horizon' encompassing all interpretation. As the famous opening injunction of *The Political Unconscious* has it – the critic must 'always historicize!'. No critic can afford to ignore the ways that history has shaped the literature written during that time. This means that a Jamesonian reading of Shakespeare's history plays would have to be aware of the historical circumstances of the late sixteenth and early seventeenth centuries. For Jameson, Shakespeare's plays embody in themselves, in their form as much as their content, the actuality of the history of Shakespeare's times: more specifically, the conflicts for social and economic power between the different classes of society that saw the old regime of aristocratic nobles begin to be superseded by a new class of trading bourgeoisie. That conflict is present in the plays that Shakespeare wrote; not so much in terms of the actual words in the drama, not on any surface level, but buried within the text, in what Jameson calls 'the political unconscious' (see Chapter 4 for a definition of this term).

Jameson does not pretend that this a straightforward project. History is not simply *there*, ready for us to access. It exists in only textual forms, forms which have to be interpreted. So interpretation is grounded, or 'horizoned' by history; but history can only be accessed by interpretation. Both interpretation and history, in other words, are involved in complex interrelations with subtle ramifications on both sides: this is a thoroughly dialectical situation, and is best explicated by dialectical criticism.

SUMMARY

Jameson's particular Marxist criticism aims both to *interpret* the books, plays, films and art that culture produces, and to explain the ways in which interpretation itself operates. In order to properly understand the world around us, Jameson thinks, we need

- A sense of the whole picture, the *totality*.
- Awareness of the way *reification* and *commodification* dominate today's culture.
- A commitment to the idea that *resistance* (or 'the negative') is essential to pleasure and to understanding.
- Comprehension that *interpretation* must be rooted in a sense of *history*.

FREUD AND LACAN

Towards *The Political Unconscious*

It is clear enough that some understanding of basic Marxist concepts is important if we want to be able to read an avowedly Marxist critic like Jameson. But there are other non-Marxist traditions that are also crucial, and foremost amongst these is the tradition that stems from the work of Sigmund Freud (1856–1939). This chapter looks at the psycho-analytical mode of criticism derived from Freud's work, and provides a vital background to a full sense of Jameson's work. It also provides an introduction to psychoanalytical theory and criticism, which has had as wide a currency in contemporary thought as Marx's ideas.

Before the *Postmodernism* book of 1990 *The Political Unconscious* was the work by which Jameson was best known. The American critic Gabriele Schwab was not alone in being 'captivated by Jameson's book, and the project it promises to outline in its suggestive title' (Schwab 1993: 83). It is likely, indeed, that for many Jameson's 'suggestive title', with its hints at a unification of Marx and Freud, has carried more weight than the actual subtle argumentation of the book itself. It is worth noting (and I note it several times in what follows) that Jameson was by no means the first to suggest linking Marx and Freud, and that thinking of him as a 'Freudian' Marxist is to misunderstand him at a basic level. Even the specific 'project' of exploring a 'political unconscious', although not exactly like Jameson's approach, was undertaken by the French thinker Pierre Macherey in his 1966 book *A*

Theory of Literary Production. Jameson's actual engagements with Freud and Freudian thinkers is broader than the soundbite suggested by the title of his 1981 book. Accordingly, in order to be able to read Jameson we need to have some sense of key concepts coined by Freud, and also by the writings of others in the Freudian tradition.

Freud is best known as the founder of the discipline of psychoanalysis, and his many writings explore the nature of consciousness in an attempt to establish a 'science' of mental analysis. Ambitions to place the psychoanalytic 'cure' of psychological illness on the same sort of scientific footing as medical 'cures' for physiological illness remain, at best, moot; but Freud's writings have had an extremely wide range of influences, and many critics have utilised his insights in the analysis of literature and culture.

There might seem to be something contradictory in pairing Marx and Freud, because there has often been thought to be a basic incompatibility in their philosophies. Putting this crudely, Freud is interested in the individual by his or herself, or in relation to a very few people (mother, father, and so on); Marx is interested in the individual in relation to the whole of society. More than this, the assumption behind the Freudian school is that society is composed of a great mass of people, whose consciousnesses have all individually been shaped by events in their personal history; whereas it is a crucial tenet of Marxism that the *opposite* to this is true – society is not determined by its individuals, but rather each individual is determined by society. As Marx put it, 'it is not the consciousness of men that determines their being, but, on the contrary, their social being that determines their consciousness' (Marx: 160). We might imagine, for instance, a person who is miserable and depressed. To this person a Freudian would be likely to say 'you are unhappy because of an internal psychological problem, because your individual psyche is unbalanced or upset in some way. To cure you we must enter into a private therapist–patient relationship where you can talk through your inner issues and so resolve them. Then you will be happy.' A Marxist, on the other hand, might well say: 'no, the truth is that you are depressed because the society you grew up in is unjust and oppressive, because you are poor, because you have no economic prospects. To cure you we must revolutionise society, because it is only in a fully just and fair society that human beings can achieve their full contented humanity. *Then* you will be happy.' This amounts to a radical conflict of emphasis, the question of whether to concentrate on the individual or on society, and there have been many thinkers who have asserted that a personal psychological approach is simply incompatible with a social political one.

Nonetheless, as Gabriele Schwab argues, when Jameson's *The Political Unconscious* first came out in 1981, it

> owed its stunning immediate success and widespread reception among literary critics to its taking up a project that emerged in the thirties...carried a lot of weight in the sixties, and was taken up again under different premises in the seventies and eighties; that of developing a theoretical framework that links Marx with Freud, politics with psychology, the collective with the individual.
>
> (Schwab, 87)

Schwab declares that 'Marxism and psychoanalysis' are, without qualification, simply 'the two most influential theoretical movements, (or as Jameson calls them 'master-narratives')' in twentieth-century life. We'll have to defer discussion of whether, and to what extent, Jameson is successful in his particular unification project until the chapter on *The Political Unconscious*. For the moment we need to establish which key Freudian ideas have been most important to Jameson's project, and that requires a brief summary of Freud's thought.

FREUD

Freud began his career as a biologist interested in the nervous system; his work as a lecturer in neuropathology introduced him to a number of patients suffering from what was then called 'hysteria' – nervous diseases where no physical cause could be discerned. Freud was increasingly drawn into the study of a range of these neurotic diseases, and as a result of work with many patients he began publishing a series of studies that developed his own highly original theories about the formation and structure of the psyche. Many of these theories are now very well known indeed. One is the emphasis on the early stages of childhood as determining later psycho-sexual life, for instance, with 'complexes' of psychological response deriving from such in-family dramas as the 'Oedipal' conflict, where the boy-child comes into conflict with his father, competing with him for the attentions of the mother. Another is Freud's invention of a 'talking cure', whereby neurotic patients work through their problems in dialogue with a therapist (the basis of contemporary psychotherapy). For our purposes here there are two aspects of Freudianism that are especially relevant to Jameson's own writings: the *unconscious* and the mechanism of *repression*.

UNCONSCIOUS

Freud postulated that any person's consciousness is made up of three elements, for which he coined the names 'id', 'ego' and 'super-ego'. The 'ego' is the 'I', that part of me that thinks 'I am me', the conscious, self-aware aspect of consciousness. The 'super-ego' is a sort of inner-policeman, a force that manifests itself in feelings of conscience, shame and guilt and acts as a break on desires and urges. The 'id', also known as the 'unconscious' or 'subconscious', is where all our primitive desires and urges come from: it is not accessible to conscious thought, but it affects all our acts. This 'unconscious' embodies the primal, instinctual drives towards gratification (for Freud, all these drives were essentially sexual, although sexual desire – libido – could be sublimated into other desires – for money, success, status, and so on). The id works outside the realms of logic or reasonableness; it just *wants*, and it doesn't care how or why. Human beings need the 'super-ego', which a person develops in early childhood, to internalise restrictions on this unconscious desiring. For instance, a baby has no super-ego; when it is hungry it wants to be fed immediately and howls if it doesn't get its way; a child knows that it must restrain its desire and wait for supper. The stratified connotations of terms such as 'conscious' and 'subconscious' make clear a certain hierarchy in Freud's structure, with the ego in the middle, presided over by the super-ego from above, and with the unconscious underground reservoir of desires and instincts of the id below. Two recent theorists, Abraham and Torok, have elaborated precisely this architectural metaphor by envisaging the 'unconscious' as akin to the crypt in an old church, underneath the building and inaccessible, but with a seepage of atmosphere coming out of it.

Although Freud insisted that a person cannot access their unconscious mind directly, it nevertheless makes itself present in a number of ways. If you hate your boss, Mr Smith, but are compelled to be polite to him (because he is your boss), you might find yourself unwittingly greeting him one day with the words 'good morning, Mr Git' – you didn't intend to call him a git, it just 'slipped out'. This is the 'Freudian slip', analysed at length in *The Psychopathology of Everyday Life* (1901); what has happened is that the unconscious (which doesn't care if you get into trouble and only knows its dislike for the man) has surreptitiously influenced your conscious mind, shifted 'Smith' into the like-sounding 'Git'. Another area where the unconscious specifically manifests itself is in dreams, and Freud's enormous book *The Interpretation of Dreams* (1900) analyses the significance of these signposts to the unconscious life (he considered dreams 'the royal road to the unconscious'). Indeed, a great deal of Freud's work was concerned with trying to fathom the workings of the unconscious because he considered any psychological problem or neurosis to be the working out in everyday life of conflicts and problems in the unconscious. One of the main jobs of the therapist is to use whatever techniques (for instance, word-association or dream analysis) to uncover what the unconscious problem of the patient is, to bring it into the conscious mind where it can be dealt with rationally.

Freud intended the notion of the 'unconscious' to apply to individuals, not to society as a whole. But there are several parallels that suggest themselves. Having in the previous chapters looked at the earlier Marxist hierarchical models of society, with an economic 'base' determining a cultural 'superstructure', we might be tempted to put alongside it a Freudian hierarchical model of personality, with a unconscious 'base' of desire determining an individual 'superstructure' of ego (modified by the actions of the superego). Here we are moving towards Jameson's own insights in *The Political Unconscious*: not that these two models are somehow equivalent, but that the Freudian model provides an accurate and fertile metaphor for examining the Marxist one. A therapist looks into the conscious mind and tries to read the hidden and coded manifestations of the unconscious that has shaped the ego in order to bring them to the surface where they can be rationally dealt with. Jameson proposes looking into aspects of the superstructure – his job is to look at cultural texts such as books and films – and to try and read the hidden and coded manifestations of the economic and political base that has shaped them. These economic and political features are often hidden in literature, but they are still there, and they can be recovered by concentrating on literary and cultural analogues of things like 'Freudian slips' or the irrationality of dreams.

So, for example, Jane Austen's novels do not, on the surface, have much to say about the class struggle for the means of production, and many critics have insisted that Austen's privileged characters live in a world of elegance and love quite removed from such grimy realities. But it is possible to focus on aspects of the fiction that may seem relatively insignificant but which reveal profound and far-reaching structures underneath. This is how a novel like *Mansfield Park* can be read by critics who spend little time on the 'surface' events of the novel (Fanny falling in love with Edmund) and instead tease out the implications of other, more marginal, aspects. There is, for example, an early scene in the novel in which the younger characters put on a *risqué* play and get into trouble. They are able to do this because the authority figure of Sir Thomas Bertram is out of the country; and he is out of the country because he is visiting his estates in the West Indies. Examining this reveals where Bertram gets his wealth – from slaves working on distant estates – and this in turn casts a particular light on the novel's obsessive working out of questions of authority and submission. In effect, the book is treated as a therapeutic patient. Freud himself discovered that neurotics undergoing psychoanalysis will often talk about anything *apart* from matters related to their neurosis, trying to avoid the unconscious cause of their pain. A critic of this Jane Austen novel would look on the bulk of the book as an elaborate avoidance tactic (although a tactic that is always, despite itself, drawing back to the central problem), designed to avoid dealing with the guilt of a privileged class whose money was derived from oppression. I should add, perhaps, that this is just an illustrative example: Jameson has not himself produced any studies of Jane Austen's novels. But he has been fascinated throughout his career with seeing beneath the apparent surfaces of capitalist life, and with reading cultural texts for what the surface reveals about the unconscious realities beneath.

This Freudian division between 'unconscious' and 'conscious' mind carries with it the distinction of 'manifest' and 'latent' meanings. Freud himself uses these terms especially when analysing dreams, his own and those of patients. The 'manifest' meaning is the surface one, what the dream appears to be about; the 'latent' meaning is what the dream is *actually* revealing about the unconscious problems and contradictions. For example, Freud records a dream by one of his patients:

> Standing back a little behind two stately palaces was a little house with closed doors. My wife led me along the piece of street up to the little house and pushed the door open; I then slipped quickly and easily into the inside of a court which rose in an incline.
>
> (Freud 1900: 521)

The *manifest* content of this dream is just what it says: this little story; but the *latent* content of the dream – what the dream symbolises – is, Freud insists, a fantasy of the dreamer having sex with his wife ('penetrating into narrow spaces and opening closed doors are among the commonest sexual symbols'). Here is another example, this time from a text rather than a dream: in the film *The Return of the Jedi* there is a scene where Jabba the Hutt, an enormous slug-like creature, has captured the beautiful Princess Leia, dressed her in a revealing bikini-costume and shackled her in chains. The 'manifest' content of this scene is just that, and makes reference to the 'evil' of Jabba and the danger that Leia is in, from which she must be rescued. But a Freudian critic would be more interested in the *latent* content of the scene, which is thoroughly sexual: an enormous phallic creature forcing himself upon a nearly naked, eroticised woman. When that same half-naked woman later kills the phallic monster by throttling its distended head with much heaving and groaning the latent subtext seems even more obvious.

Freud talks about the need to 'avoid confusing' the 'dream as it is retained in my memory [the manifest content] with the relevant material discovered by analysing it [the latent content]' (Freud 1986: 88–9). For a cultural critic this distinction is even more marked: texts themselves – the manifest content – are often very different from their 'unconscious' or latent 'relevant material'. Indeed, as Jameson notes on several occasions, the relationship between manifest and latent content is often inverted or upside down. 'Freud has taught us,' he observes, 'that the manifest totality of a fantasy or a dream' (a category Jameson wants to expand to include a variety of 'cultural artefacts') '...is not a reliable guide, save by inversion and negation, to the meaning of the latent content: dreams of dead loved ones proving in reality to be happy wish fulfilments about something utterly unrelated' (*P*: 383).

Accordingly texts need to be read 'against the grain', as the phrase goes, which is to say to be critically analysed in ways that might seem counter-intuitive, to reveal the really significant features lurking in their unconscious (an example might be the reading of Austen's *Mansfield Park* I sketched in above). This is not an arbitrary process, of course, but one always controlled by an awareness of the forces that shape the passage from unconscious to conscious, from latent to manifest – for Jameson, forces of history.

The reason for this apparent disparity between unconscious and conscious has to do with the second key concept of Freud that Jameson draws on, that of repression.

REPRESSION

For Freud, 'repression' was a kind of psychological defence mechanism, whereby thoughts, responses or impulses that are unacceptable or too painful for the conscious mind to cope with are 'buried' in the subconscious. This is a form of denial, a squashing down of whatever it is that makes the individual feel anxious in an attempt to get rid of it, disposing of it into the 'dustbin' of the id. But, crucially for Freud's technique, things repressed into the subconscious do not simply go away: they – inevitably – return. This 'return of the repressed' can take a number of forms, but a common one is precisely the neuroses that Freud began his career examining. For example: a person is terrified of spiders, so scared that he is reduced to a gibbering wreck every time he encounters one. There is no actual basis for this fear (the person lives in London, where none of the spiders are poisonous); rather it is the *manifest* expression of a greater, *latent* fear, a fear that produces so much anxiety that the man has repressed it completely. Freud might argue that this real fear is the fear of castration, which he considered to be something all boy-children have to come to terms with in their developments. The painful thoughts and emotions associated with this fear of castration are so enormous that they are repressed, and when they return they have been changed by the subconscious (if they came back unchanged they would simply be repressed again), altered – for instance – according to the associative logic of dreams, where the spider becomes a *symbol* for the anxiety. By revealing that the neurotic fear of spiders is actually a coded fear for something else, the therapist can bring the anxiety from the unconscious into the conscious mind, where the patient can get it in proportion and deal with it.

In an essay published in 1975, six years before *The Political Unconscious*, Jameson can be seen working his way towards what he calls 'Freudo-Marxism' or 'the relationship of Freud's own object of study, namely sexuality, to the cultural phenomena that concern us'. He wonders about the dismissive responses many Westerners have to non-Western art and culture (from African tribal art to the 'little red book' of Mao Zedong). 'I will suggest...' he says

> that our first task is not to persuade ourselves of the validity for us of these
> alien or primitive art forms, but rather to attempt to measure the whole extent
> of our boredom with them and our almost visceral refusal of what can only be
> (to our own jaded tastes) the uninventive simplicity and repetition, the litur-
> gical slowness and predictability.
>
> ('Beyond the Cave', *IT2*: 117–18)

This is a startling strategy; almost a perverse one. It seems, quite apart from anything else, impolite to watch (say) a Japanese Noh drama and to concentrate on the ways in which the piece bores and alienates us, instead of trying to convince ourselves that it probably *is* good, that we *ought* to find it interesting. It sounds philistine to suggest that a Western critic has a duty to concentrate on the sensations of boredom and alienation, but Jameson has a particular reason for his argument, and he invokes the Freudian concept of repression to explain himself.

> The notion of repression is by no means as dramatic as it might at first appear,
> for in psychoanalytical theory, whatever its origins and whatever the final
> effect of repression on the personality, its symptoms and its mechanisms are
> quite the opposite of violence, and are nothing quite so much as looking away,
> forgetting, ignoring, losing interest. Repression is reflexive, that is, it aims not
> only at removing a particular object from consciousness, but also and above all,
> at doing away with the traces of the removal as well, at repressing the very
> memory of the intent to repress. This is the sense in which the boredom I
> evoked a moment ago may serve as a powerful hermeneutic instrument: it
> marks the spot where something painful is buried, it invites us to reawaken all
> the anguished hesitation, the struggle of the subject to avert his or her eyes
> from the thought with which brutal arms insists on confronting him.
>
> ('Beyond the Cave', *IT2*: 118)

In other words, we can *learn* from our boredom, about things such as the way we have been repressing our fuller responses to art from outside our own cultural traditions. This becomes an interesting account of 'boredom' (something which has not been very extensively theorised); like the fear of spiders in a patient undergoing analysis, this negative response is not *just* a negative response; it is the symptom of something deeper and more significant buried in the 'political uncon-scious'. In other words, Jameson wants to connect our negativity to 'foreign' art with the ways capitalist society has demonised and exploited the 'other' of Africa and Asia; this trauma of exploitation is buried, and it is only at our moments of negative response to manifestations of these cultures that we can start to uncover the truth of the matter. If a Western audience had just enjoyed the African or Asian art, they would not have been confronted with the 'strangeness', the 'otherness' of African and Asian culture; there would have been no need to begin thinking about the history of imperialism and exploitation that underlies the history of the West's interventions in Africa and Asia.

This points to another reason why Jameson is drawn to the Freudian model. Freud's models of consciousness were derived from, and were used in curing, sick and neurotic people; he was mostly describing a series of psychic *pathologies*, or illnesses. It is an interesting feature of psychological illness that patients are often very insistent that they are *not* ill, and emphatically deny that there is anything wrong, despite all manner of debilitating neurotic or psychosomatic symptoms (nightmares, irrational terrors, neurotic compulsions, and so on). From Jameson's Marxist perspective, this becomes a description of *society in general*. Capitalism insists it is in rude health and declares it will just carry on, despite a series of clear pathological symptoms (widespread poverty, oppression, misery). The Marxist critic can act as a sort of social therapist, exploring the areas where the painful problems of modern society have been 'buried' or repressed.

LACAN

Freud himself stands at the head of a rich tradition of Freudian analysis, and various thinkers and psychological practitioners have expanded and explored his insights. One such is Jacques Lacan (1901–81), a French theorist, who has little currency in the Anglo-American psycho-analytical world but who has been highly influential in the worlds of literary and cultural criticism, and on Jameson in particular. One reason why Lacan has had so little impact on the world of psychoanalysis is that his writing style is ferociously difficult, possibly the most obscure and challenging of all the 'difficult' theoretical writers (Jameson included). But that notwithstanding, one of the reasons why he has been so influential amongst literary critics is that he combined Freud's insights into the psyche with the linguistic and structuralist discourses of Ferdinand de Saussure (1857–1913) and Roman Jakobson (1896–1982). Structuralism analysed language in terms of systems of signification. Jameson's *The Prison House of Language* (1972) provides a fairly critical account of the structuralist movement in the human sciences (his problem, roughly, is that structuralists like Saussure were too abstract, too removed from the 'real' world of history and society). But Jameson concedes the huge influence and importance of the 'doctrine of the sign' that Saussure introduced.

To summarise this very rapidly: in place of the old fuzzy model whereby a 'word' refers to a 'thing', Saussure introduced the notion of words as signs, a combination of a *signifier* (for instance, the word 'tree') and a *signified* (the item to which the signifier refers). It is conventional to represent this model with the following diagram:

$$\frac{\text{signifier}}{\text{signified}} = \text{sign}$$

The point about this shift is that the word tree does not produce its meaning by being connected somehow to any *thing*, to any particular tree, or even to any ideal notion of a tree in the mind. Instead, we understand what the word 'tree' means with reference to a system of relations; this system of relations is only a convention, and is indeed mostly arbitrary. A popular structuralist argument involves the sign system of traffic lights, where the red light instructs drivers to stop, the amber to prepare to go and the green to go. A driver will 'read' these signs:

$$\frac{\text{signifier ('red light')}}{\text{signified ('stop the car')}}$$

This sign can only be properly read within the system of signification, taught to drivers, whereby red is taken to mean stop. The connection between signifier and signified is arbitrary, red has simply been chosen as the colour to represent 'stop' (in revolutionary China in the 1960s the code was changed so that 'red' became the colour for 'go' – because 'red' was seen as the revolutionary socialist colour of progress and change. It can be added that, provided drivers understand the change, this new system of signification works just as well). This structuralist system is most richly applied, of course, in language, where all the words function as arbitrary signifiers for various signifieds. Depending on context, then, 'pig' might signify a porcine animal, a

greedy individual, a bar of iron and so on: at the same time, this semiotic (which is to say, sign) system functions by *difference*. Pig means pig
in part because it does not mean 'dog', 'cow' or other such words; and
in part it generates its meaning by lexical difference, so that 'pig'
differs from 'dig', 'wig', and so on.

Structuralism represents a very detailed body of scholarship to
summarise so crudely. It is important for Lacan, though – and, through
him, for Jameson – because of the Lacanian belief that the Freudian
ego does not exist as some brute fact of nature like eyes or legs, but
rather as a *sign*, a system that only comes into existence in a signifying
system like language. According to Lacan, we cannot say that the ego
is, we have to say that it comes into being through a process of signification. Becoming a person, for Lacan, is similar to learning a language:
it involves entry into a signifying system based, in structuralist terms,
on the arbitrariness of the signifier/signified relation, and also on the
signifying practice of difference. We grow up by positioning ourselves
in the pre-existing 'languages' of, say, gender, by positioning ourselves
as 'male' or 'female', as 'son' or 'daughter', and so on. As Raman
Seldon puts it:

> Lacan restates Freud's theories in the language of Saussure. Essentially,
> unconscious processes are identified with the unstable signifier...For example,
> when a subject enters the symbolic order and accepts a *position* as son or
> daughter, a certain linking of signifier and signified is made possible. However
> 'I' am never where I think; 'I' stands at the axis of signifier and signified, never
> able to give my position a full presence. In Lacan's version of the sign, the
> signifier 'slides' beneath a signifier which 'floats'.

> (Seldon: 82)

In other words, Lacan's version of the self is that it is a fiction, it is
something rather like a novel or a poem in the continual process of
being composed: the ego is not stable and settled, but *un*stable, in a
constant process of flux, being 'written' by experience and attitude, or
indeed being constantly rewritten and written over, propelled by the
forces of the unconscious. It is easy to see why this conception appeals
to literary critics (and also, perhaps, why its deliberate slipperiness has
alienated psychiatrists and psychological healthcare professionals).
Arguing, as Lacan does, that 'the unconscious is structured like a
language' suggests that the people best able to analyse the processes of

the psyche are people skilled in reading languages and texts. It also fits nicely in with the ideas of deconstruction, whereby texts themselves (even though 'novels' aren't alive and changing in the same way that a human being is) are nonetheless involved in the same process of constant 'rewriting' and flux. For both Lacanians and deconstructivists, the relationship between signifier and signified is characterised by sliding and floating. As Jameson observes, for Lacan 'consciousness is something on the order of a "shifter" in linguistics', it is a term that 'shifts' its 'object of reference with context' (*PHL*: 138).

Lacan reconfigured Freud's notions of the development of the individual along these lines, mapping out three 'categories' of psychological apprehension, or stages in individual growth, which he called 'Imaginary', 'Symbolic' and 'Real'.

'IMAGINARY', 'SYMBOLIC' AND 'REAL'

Lacan theorised three different arenas or conceptual spaces in which the individual psyche operates. The first of these is the 'Imaginary', so called because its currency is images; this develops first of all, when the young child (6 to 18 months) recognises its 'image' in the mirror, and it remains a part of individual consciousness throughout life. The Imaginary is a polymorphous assemblage of fantasies and images, not yet structured by the 'symbolic' of language. Since it dates from before the entry into the 'symbolic' that produces the ego and its sense of itself, the Imaginary makes little distinction between self and other. In Jameson's words, the Imaginary is 'a uniquely determined configuration of space – one that is not yet organised around the individuation of my own personal body, or differentiated hierarchically according to the perspectives of my own central point of view, but that nonetheless swarms with bodies and forms intuited in a different way' (*IT1*: 85).

The apprehension of language introduces the 'symbolic' order. Here the ego develops, structured like a language according to the semiotic principles of the structuralist analyses of language, by difference and the arbitrariness of semiotic connections. Jameson describes it pithily: 'the Symbolic Order is that realm into which the child emerges, out of a biological namelessness [the Imaginary], when he gradually acquires language. It is impersonal, or superpersonal, but it is also that which permits the very sense of identity itself to come into being. Consciousness, personality, the subject are, therefore...secondary phenomena which are determined by the vaster structure of language itself, or of the Symbolic' (*PHL*: 130). A surrealist painting, in which a variety of visual images are thrown together without the structure of language to explain them, functions – affects us, moves us – on the level of the imaginary: although once we begin to try and explain why we like the painting, we shift our analysis into the Symbolic.

The final term in the triad, the 'Real' is what its name suggests: it is the reality outside the subject's consciousness. For Lacan, 'real life' or 'the real world' can never actually be apprehended, because the act of perceiving reality necessarily filters it through consciousness where it enters into the psychological logic of the Imaginary and the Symbolic. The Real, then, exists outside symbolisation, outside language, and more than this it *resists* symbolisation. An example of the Real, for Lacan, would be the primary Object that the subject desires – the mother's body, taken away so long ago. In place of this unobtainable Real the subject discovers a number of symbolic signifiers that relate to the Real: these things (a sexualised body, a consumer object) constitute the unobtainable aspect of otherness, *l'objet petit a* (abbreviated by Lacan to a small 'a', which stands for *autre*, the French for 'other').

Lacan characterised the development of the individual as the entry into several 'stages'. To begin with, infants in the womb makes no distinction between themselves, their mother, or the world around them. After birth infants still live in this conceptual world, where they do not know where they end and their mother's breast begins, but now experience is sometimes fragmented in ways it was not before (because the breast is sometimes taken away). All adult desires, Lacan theorised, reflect a 'lack' of some kind, and all these 'lacks' go back, fundamentally, to the acute sense of lack an infant feels when its unified bliss is broken by this fragmentation. The 'self' must be developed to deal with the anxieties of this fragmentation, and it starts to form itself at what Lacan called 'the mirror stage', a stage of human development that takes place some time between six and eighteen months. What happens during this stage is that infants, for the first time, recognise themselves in the mirror. Actually, this is not a 'recognition, but a *mis*recognition, because what the child sees is not itself but an image of itself which is confused with itself. This mirror phase constitutes the entry of the individual into the *imaginary* order, because it begins a process where consciousness is structured according to images. With the acquisition of language later in the child's development, consciousness moves into a further order, the *symbolic*, where the structures of language enable the ego to call itself into being, to define itself by the semiotic processes of difference and slippery signification that characterise language as a whole. The 'symbolic' order is the place where culture (for instance, literature) takes place, and where individual subjects develop a sense of themselves, of their 'I'. One of the interesting implications of these ideas of Lacan's is that language actively constructs who we are; that without language it would not be possible to develop an ego, a self-aware consciousness at all. The third stage in the Lacanian development of the individual has to do with the encounter with the other. At the beginning the infant and child is concerned with its own sense of self; at a later stage, the developing consciousness transfers its desire – its original 'lack' of the mother's body – onto other individuals around them. For Lacan, individuals seek the others they desire, but by doing so they can never actually satisfy their desire because these others are merely standing in for the real desire, for the absent body of the mother that can never be replaced. In his language, desire is a pursuit of the fixed signified ('the real') in which the desired object is constantly sliding into a signifier (for instance, a particular person, a material possession, and so on). A woman falling in love with a beautiful man, or a man desiring a sports car, are actually desiring symbolic *signifiers*: these signifiers relate to the signified (the real, the body of the mother) but – as is the way with signs – they can never actually apprehend or fix the signified. Desire involves 'the incessant sliding of the signified under the signifier' (Lacan: 154).

The order of the Lacanian 'Real' has been theorised by Althusser by placing it in a Marxist context. In *The Political Unconscious* Jameson discusses the way 'Althusser's anteleogical formula for history (neither a subject nor a telos)' – where 'telos' means an 'end' or a 'purpose' and Althusser's 'anteleogical formula' is an insistence on *not* reading history as if it were a single organic unity (see above p. 30) – the way 'Althusser's anteleogical formula for history (neither a subject nor a telos)' is based on 'Lacan's notion of the Real as that which "resists symbolization altogether"' (*PU*: 34–5). In other words, for a writer like Jameson, Lacan has two interesting implications: one is that the subject is seen not as an organ that 'naturally' grows with the growth of the body, but rather as a textual site, constantly being written and rewritten, shifting in meaning and fragile. For a Marxist, clearly, the subject is 'written' by society and history, and a Lacanian sense of the subject as a site of conflicting meaning–production instead of a smooth little pebble of unified identity allows for more trenchant and fertile analyses of exactly those forces that 'write' people into being – family, society, culture, and so on. The second interesting notion that Jameson has drawn from Lacan is a sense of 'history' as 'the Real', as something which cannot be directly apprehended but only known through its symbolic (and, perhaps, imaginary) manifestations. This allows for a much more complex and penetrating analysis of key Marxist concepts than the old 'vulgar' Marxist approach, where history was a straightforward matter of class struggle.

JAMESON, CRITICISM AND LACAN

In his important essay 'Imaginary and Symbolic in Lacan' (1977), Jameson summarises and analyses what Lacanian thinking has to offer the project of criticism in general, and a Marxist criticism in particular. For Jameson, it is Lacan's two categories of the Imaginary and the Symbolic, and their differing if interlocking range of implications, that are most illuminating: 'the distinction between the Imaginary and the Symbolic, and the requirement that a given analysis be able to do justice to the qualitative gap between them, may prove to be an invaluable instrument for measuring the range or the limits of a particular way of thinking' (*IT1*: 99). He gives an example of what he means by invoking the common critical tactic of analysing a text by listing and analysing its 'imagery', something critics of poetry are especially prone to do. But according to Jameson, the point of picking out the imagery of the sea in Matthew Arnold, or the imagery of blood in Shakespeare's *Macbeth*, is not to illustrate the 'production of imagery' but rather 'its mastery and control' (*IT1*: 99). This is because the image is the material of the Imaginary, and a Lacanian analysis must always be aware of the ways that the Symbolic – language – has overlaid the chaos of the Imaginary with structure and order, 'repressing' the earlier traces.

> Only by grasping images…in this way, as that trace of the Imaginary, of sheer
> private or physiological experience, which has undergone the sea change of the

> Symbolic, can criticism of this kind recover a vital and hermeneutic relation-
> ship to the literary text.

(IT1: 99)

It is too simplistic to identify the Imaginary as visual and the Symbolic as verbal (visual experience can be very highly structured, and verbal experience can be relatively free from structure); nor is it a case of 'repudiating the Imaginary and substituting the Symbolic for it – as though the one were "bad" and the other "good" – but rather of elaborating a method that can articulate both whilst preserving their radical discontinuity with each other' (*IT1*: 101). Jameson suggests two approaches to criticism that he thinks have privileged the one term over the other. First, there is criticism that stresses the schizophrenic fragmentation of texts, or which – like Bertolt Brecht's theories about anti-realist theatre – 'can best be understood as an attempt to block Imaginary investment and thereby dramatise the problematical relationship between the observing subject and the Symbolic Order' (*IT1*: 102). In other words, Jameson sees Brecht as trying to show up the logic of the Symbolic, the structures or ordering and control, as the same forces that tend to oppress individual subjects. For critics like this (Jameson also mentions Foucault and Deleuze) the Symbolic Order is too straightforwardly identified with oppressive power, and the Imaginary too easily assimilated to revolutionary freedom. At the other end of the scale, Jameson points out 'the overestimation of the Symbolic itself' in the 'development of semiotics' and the various structuralist approaches to criticism of critics like Ferdinand de Saussure and Roman Jakobson. An analysis of a text purely in terms of the binary patterns of its signifying practices will be able to see that text only in terms of the Symbolic of language, and 'its blind spots may therefore be expected to be particularly instructive as to the problems of the insertion of the Imaginary into the model of a Symbolic system' (*IT1*: 102). He is suggesting that Structuralism is useful, but will be blind to the irrational, Imaginary aspects of art.

Jameson's preferred approach, as might be expected, argues a more 'Marxist' and dialectical approach to the question. To this end, he comes back to the Lacanian concept of 'the Real', and applies a thoroughly Marxist definition. Only 'the Real' can 'put an end to the Imaginary opposition into which our previous discussion of Lacan's two orders has risked falling again and again'. But how can we identify what the Real is when, as Lacan himself says, the Real is 'what resists symbolization absolutely'? (*IT1*: 104). Jameson is not dismayed by Lacan's evasions.

> Nonetheless, it is not terribly difficult to say what is meant by the Real in Lacan. It is simply history itself; and if for psychoanalysis the history in question here is obviously enough the history of the subject, the resonance of the word suggests that a confrontation between this particular materialism and the historical materialism of Marx can no longer be postponed.
>
> (*IT1*: 104)

For Jameson, 'History' is the benchmark, the thing in which all proper criticism should be grounded. This means that a reading of a text (say, Joseph Conrad's short novel *Heart of Darkness*, 1902) needs to be constantly oriented towards history, not only the history of the Congo in the nineteenth century but also the history of Conrad's own life and times; and not just the accumulation of brute facts of historical record, but the way 'history in its other sense, as story and storytelling' (*IT1*: 107) shapes the narrative of Conrad's tale. As the Lacanian Real History itself defies Symbolization, it can never be grasped *in itself* in any text; but Jameson makes the point that there is always some *version* of history in every text, just as all of us carries some notion of what the Real World outside our consciousnesses is. Critical analysis can therefore proceed, providing we 'distinguish between our own narrative of history – whether psychoanalytical or political – and the Real itself, which our narratives can only approximate in asymptotic [i.e. diagonal, oblique] fashion and which "resists symbolization absolutely"' (*IT1*: 107). Examples of Jameson reading specific novels (by Balzac, Gissing and Conrad) this way are to be found in *The Political Unconscious* (chapters 3, 4 and 5), and are discussed below in Chapter 4. But we can say that, in practical terms, what this actually means is that Jameson sees the shifting stages of capitalist history over the last two hundred years as the 'Real' determinant of the forms literature and culture have taken. So, the rise of industrialisation lies behind 'nineteenth-century realism', imperial capitalism at the end of the nineteenth century and early twentieth century is behind 'modernism' and post-industrial capitalism is behind today's 'postmodernism'.

Jameson's assertion, quoted above, that a 'confrontation' between Lacan's psychoanalytical sense of the Real and the historical materialist conception of the same term in the Marxist tradition 'can no longer be postponed' brings us back to the issue of unifying Marxist and Freudian perspectives. In 'Imaginary and Symbolic in Lacan', Jameson praises Lacan for providing precisely the tools necessary to link these twin discourses. To begin with, he says:

> Marxism and psychoanalysis indeed present a number of striking analogies of structure with each other, as a checklist of their major themes can testify: the relation of theory and practice; the resistance of false consciousness and the problem as to its opposite (is it knowledge or truth? science or individual certainty?); the role and risks of the concept of a 'midwife' of truth, whether analyst or [politically revolutionary] vanguard party; the reappropriation of an alienated history and the function of narrative; the question of desire and value and of the nature of 'false desire'; the paradox of the end of the revolutionary process, which, like analysis, must surely be considered 'interminable' rather than 'terminable'; and so forth.
>
> (*IT1*: 106)

More than this, both Marxism and Freudianism, 'these two nineteenth-century "philosophies"' have come under attack for what Jameson calls their 'naive semanticism'. Semantics is the study of meanings; and by 'naive semanticism' I take it that Jameson is talking about a naive belief that the true meanings of things can be easily determined through a proper understanding of the economic base or the psychological unconscious. But Lacan supplies the absence that brings both terms together: 'a concept of language'. It is his particular version of how language works, and how it constructs our identities, that makes Lacan 'therefore in this perspective an exemplary figure' (*IT1*: 106). By seeing the construction of the individual subject as an entry into *language*, and as oriented forever towards something – the Real – that cannot be reached, Lacan has described a paradigm that also describes the way, from a Marxist perspective, society determines the consciousness of its individuals, grounded at all times in the unapprehendable 'reality' of history.

I hope this goes some way towards suggesting that Jameson's own engagement with Freudianism is not a simplistic mapping of the one realm onto the structures of Marxist thought. Jameson himself often makes gentle sideways swipes at a too unsophisticated marriage of Freud and Marx. Although the 'Frankfurt School' (a group of Marxist thinkers that included Adorno, Horkheimer and Marcuse, among others) is sometimes credited with an attempt to link Freud and Marx,

Jameson can only detect 'a kind of supplementary social psychology' where 'repression and the damaged subject' are seen as the direct 'results of the exchange process and the dynamics of capitalism' (*LM*: 26). This is much too crude an approach for Jameson. To point to an individual and ask 'why is she depressed?' (or to pick out a single character in a novel and say 'how do you explain her psyche?') is, in a sense, to ask the wrong question. Instead, Jameson is (in critic Steven Hemling's words) attempting a 'criticism capable of achieving mediations between the social and the individual that could draw on psychoanalysis without reducing the social to the categories of individual psychology' (Hemling: 1).

SUMMARY

Of the many aspects of Freud's theory taken up and developed by Freudian thinkers like Lacan, there are a few that are especially important for an understanding of Jameson:

- The Freudian three-part model of consciousness, 'unconsciousness', 'ego' and 'super-ego'. In particular, the *unconscious* part of the mind, where desire, or libido, governs before it is modified by the super-ego.
- The processes of *repression* that occur when the super-ego tries to block out some of the impulses of the unconscious.
- Lacan's refinement of the Freudian model, whereby *language* becomes seen as the way the unconscious is ordered.
- Lacan's own three-part model of individual development, the pre-language *Imaginary*, the more structured *Symbolic*, and the ultimate *Real*. Where other criticism has been based on the imaginary or the symbolic, for Jameson the 'Real' is history, and should be the principle of criticism.

Both psychoanalysis and Marxism are crucial to Jameson's project of interpretation, his work as a critic. One of the most influential things he has done is to find a way of combining the seemingly opposed ways of thinking that 'Freud' and 'Marx' represent. This is the project of his book *The Political Unconscious* which is the subject of the next chapter.

4

THE POLITICAL UNCONSCIOUS

We have already, in the last chapter, looked at some of the basic premises underlying Jameson's 1981 book, *The Political Unconscious*. As was
mentioned there, the project of coming up with some unified theory
that takes advantage of these two hugely powerful and influential theories – Marxism and Freudianism – had occupied various thinkers
throughout the twentieth century. Jameson was by no means the first
person to attempt that particular synthesis. Nor is *The Political
Unconscious* actually a 'unification' of dialectical materialism and
psychoanalysis (which is to say its title does *not* translate as '*The Marxist
Freudianism*'). Jameson does draw on Freud's work, particularly as
interpreted by Lacan, but the whole is firmly located within a specifically Marxist framework. Indeed, he is quite firm in stating his opinion
that Marxism, as a philosophy, possesses 'primacy' amongst other ways
of thinking and doing criticism: 'Marxism is here conceived as that
"untranscendable horizon" that subsumes such apparently antagonistic
or incommensurable critical operations…at once cancelling and
preserving them.' These other non-Marxist critical operations (in addition to Freud, Jameson draws on thinkers such as Northrop Frye and
Greimas) are 'preserved' because Jameson reserves a place for them
within the framework of Marxism; but they are 'cancelled' because, in
the final analysis, he considers that Marxism supersedes them.

Some readers of *The Political Unconscious* have been frustrated that

Jameson spends so much time in this book worrying away at the specifics of Marxist hermeneutics rather than straightforwardly setting out his concept of 'the political unconscious'. Certainly, the reader will look in vain for any definition of this presumably central concept in Jameson's book, which may or may not be seen as a good thing. Geoff Bennington (whose deconstructivist affiliations render him unlikely to approve of Jameson's approach to begin with) has criticised the book, arguing that the sheer density and clottedness of Jameson's approach, his florid style, the footnotes, digressions, lengthy preambles, and so on, merely get in the way of his professed political agenda. Bennington suggests that everything in this book is delayed and put off, including any definition of what a 'political unconscious' is supposed to be (Bennington 1994: 74–87). On the other hand, Dominick LaCapra praises Jameson's book for the richness and suggestiveness of this central concept, a richness preserved by the fact that it 'is defined – insofar as it is at all – only by its multiple uses' (LaCapra 1985: 236).

That said, the Freudian concept of the unconscious *is* crucial to Jameson's project here. In his earlier essays, Jameson had sketched out what he took to be valuable and what redundant in earlier attempts to graft Freudian and Marxist insights together. In his important essay on Lacan, for instance ('Imaginary and Symbolic in Lacan', 1977) he suggests that 'the synthesis of Marx and Freud projected by the Frankfurt School' of Adorno, Horkheimer, and others, 'has not worn well'

> often seeming mechanical in those moments in Adorno's literary or musical studies when a Freudian scheme is perfunctorily introduced into a discussion of cultural or formal history.
>
> (*IT*1:79)

It is not enough, in other words, simply to 'bolt on' aspects of Freudian thinking – to introduce Freudian terms or methods of analysis at odd moments as and when it suits you. A properly synthesised methodology is essential first. On the other hand, there is one feature of Frankfurt School 'Freudo-Marxism' that Jameson considers fruitful:

> What remains powerful in this part of their work, however, is a more global model of repression which, borrowed from psychoanalysis, provides the underpinnings for their sociological vision of the total system ... of late capitalism.
>
> (*IT*1:79)

For 'repression' see Chapter 3, but as Jameson points out Adorno and Horkheimer are taking their model of repression not so much from 'clinical Freudianism' but 'rather from *Civilisation and its Discontents*' – the Freud text that is most specifically about society in general. In that classic – and short – study, Freud traces the increasing levels of 'civilisation' in human history, and sees a simultaneous increase in the repression, with according neurosis and unhappiness, that inevitably accompanies it. In a primitive society, people had fewer restrictions: they were able to follow through with more of their instincts and desires. But 'civilisation' involves increasingly sophisticated rules and behaviours governing behaviour. In order to fit into contemporary 'civilised' society, individuals are made to feel guilty and ashamed about their desires for untrammelled sex or their spontaneous violent anger towards others. These unacceptable feelings are accordingly repressed into the unconscious, from where they return in altered forms as neuroses and fetishes.

Sometimes Jameson seems to be toying with exactly the sort of analogical observation of parallels between Marxism and Freudianism that he elsewhere warns against. In his 1973 essay on Max Weber, 'The Vanishing Mediator', he ponders the posture of 'Romantic despair' associated particularly with Byron and other Romantic poets, in which 'the sufferer withdraws completely from the world, to sit apart in a post of Byronic malediction…To such a state, the essential gesture of which is *refusal*, either heroic or dejected, the description as well as the diagnosis made by Freud for the condition he called "melancholy" might most fittingly apply' (*IT2*: 6). According to Freud, melancholy resulted from the loss of an external object that the libido or sex drive had fixated upon: this need not be an actual sexual partner, of course; for Freud the libido was the general currency of the unconscious and could be invested in anything. Jameson concludes with a move to the socio-political: 'we may perhaps over hastily suggest that the object thus mourned by the Romantics was the aristocratic world itself, which even the Restoration was unable to bring back to life'. The qualifying phrase ('perhaps over hastily') doesn't actually preserve the sentiment from invoking a crude parallelism of Marxism and Freudianism.

But it is the fundamental premise of *The Political Unconscious* that there are useful connections to be made between Freud and Marx when it comes to the business of interpretation. In particular, Jameson accepts a Freudian model of surface and depth, something that puts him at odds (again) with many post-structuralist thinkers, who would deny exactly that model. In essence, Jameson argues that we need to treat texts as if they were psychiatric patients; that the *surface* meanings of texts are not necessarily reliable indicators to the important stuff, to what is really going on *underneath the surface*. A critic, by paying attention to the 'symptoms' of the text, can access the unconscious 'reality'. Partly this means a particular attention to *form* rather than content; as Jameson has already argued in *Marxism and Form*, textual form (in *The Political Unconscious* he is especially interested in *narrative* form) embodies ideological significance just as much, or perhaps even more than, the content. But the three terms that orient Jameson's approach in this work have to do with linking together these different Freud-style levels of the text: narrative, mediation and history. To put it in a sentence: the surface narration usefully mediates the unconscious reality of the text's relationship with history. These are terms I now need to define.

HISTORY AND MEDIATION

The Political Unconscious starts off with a lengthy chapter on 'Interpretation' that sets out the terms of Jameson's particular engagement with Marxism and Freudianism. This is followed by chapters that provide more specific readings of particular forms, a chapter on 'Magical Narratives' that looks at the 'Romance' form, and chapters that analyse novels by nineteenth-century novelists Honore de Balzac (1799–1850), George Gissing (1857–1903) and the modernist writer Joseph Conrad (1857–1924) in turn. We will come to these analyses soon, but for the moment we need to examine what Jameson is saying in his first chapter. Some of this has been covered earlier. Specifically, *The Political Unconscious* marks an advance over an earlier Marxist study such as *Marxism and Form* in its relative openness to the ideas of Althusser and the school of deconstructivist Marxism that is associated with his name. No longer so unambiguously Hegelian, Jameson spends much of the first chapter of *The Political Unconscious* picking out those aspects of the Althusserian approach that seem to him useful (without ever actually endorsing Althusserianism altogether). This is a little tedious for many readers, and has already been covered in part in Chapter 1. What is more appealing, for our purposes here, is the way

Jameson establishes the twin dynamics of his particular approach to criticism. This can be boiled down to the invocation of two terms: history and mediation.

We have touched on Jameson's repeated commitment to a historical criticism many times in this study. For him, as we saw earlier (pp. 67) history is the Lacanian 'Real', the ultimate thing which, although it can never actually be apprehended directly by us does exist in textual form, for instance in the shape of novels he looks at by Balzac, Gissing and Conrad. No criticism is worthwhile for Jameson unless it is alert to the shaping determinism of history; no critical account of the novel will work unless it understands the way the specific historical circumstances of the eighteenth and nineteenth centuries shaped the development of that particular form. By history, Jameson, as a Marxist, does not mean 'the doings of Kings and Princes'; he means the class struggles and economic evolution of society that saw the rise of the bourgeoisie in the eighteenth and nineteenth centuries, a rise which is directly embodied in the 'bourgeoisie' form of literature, the novel. Speaking crudely, Jameson follows socialist economist Ernest Mandel (1923–95) in attributing shifting phases to the development of capitalism, from early capitalism, through industrial capitalism (in the nineteenth century) and imperial capitalism (in the early twentieth century), through to 'late capitalism' of the present day. This history is always present in art and culture, and the critic needs to be aware of this. The very first words of *The Political Unconscious* declare this unambiguously:

> Always historicize! This slogan – the one absolute and we may even say 'transhistorical' imperative of all dialectical thought – will unsurprisingly turn out to be the moral of *The Political Unconscious* as well.
>
> (*PU*: 9)

In a word, this is what the 'political unconscious' *is*: it is history, present in every text but rarely evidently so. The fact that *Alice in Wonderland* or Shakespeare's love sonnets are actually 'about' history is a feature of the unconscious of these texts, and needs to be recovered by the attentive critic.

The reason why Jameson considers it so crucial to attend to literature is that he sees in this material one of the most crucial forms of *mediation* in current society, and much of the introductory chapter defines exactly what his sense of that term is.

MEDIATION

It is one of the tenets of Marxism along with many other philosophies that human existence is not apprehended directly, but is *mediated* or accessed via some middle mechanism or concept. An example would be a reader who does not speak Ancient Greek but who wants to read Homer's *Iliad*. She cannot read this poem directly, but she *can* read it if her reading is 'mediated' through a translation of Homer; here the translation is the mediation. In a Marxist context, examples are more likely to be social, perhaps as a critique of industrialisation and urbanisation. So (the argument might go) at one time structures and systems like 'the village', 'the family' or 'the church' could mediate between an individual and his or her experience of the world, providing coherence and valuable meaning to existence. Modern counterparts of these mediations, however, like 'the city', 'science' or 'fandom' do not operate with this organic coherence and are liable to criticism. In a sense it could be argued that the supreme mediator today is money; Marx himself talks about the way money tends to mediate between subject and object, people and things, with various damaging consequences. It is important in Marxism to pay attention to these mediating structures, since it is through them that people make sense of themselves and their place in the world. Several Marxists have stressed the importance of art and literature as precisely one such key mediator. Jameson's definition of mediation ('the relationship between the levels or instances, and the possibility of adapting analyses and findings from one level to another' *PU*: 39) seems dry and a little obscure, but is referring to the same thing. One of the key arguments in *The Political Unconscious* is that it is narrative, story-forms and plots that play a dominant role in mediating individual experience and social totality, according to a process of what he calls *transcoding* – the translating into an accepted code (which consists of certain narrative patterns and expectations) of social and historical reality to make it accessibly mediated for the individual.

According to Satya P. Mohanty, 'one of the main contributions of *The Political Unconscious* to Marxist literary and cultural studies is its substantive theory of narrative as a mediational category' (Mohanty 1997: 101). For Jameson 'mediation is the classical dialectical term for the establishment of relationships between, say, the formal analysis of a work of art and its social ground, or between the internal dynamics of the political state and its economic base' (*PU*: 39). Mediation is 'dialectical' because it has to go back and forth between two perhaps very different (or even opposed) objects: so, a mediatory reading of Jane Austen's *Mansfield Park* needs to encounter both the surface level of the novel (its love-story conventionalities) and its 'unconscious' social reading (its position in the historical ground of the rise of the bourgeoisie, with the associated issues of owning property and proper authority). More than this, though, Jameson's 'dialectical mediation' has a larger role than just the reading of specific literary texts. 'Marxist criticism' is for him the proper *mediation* between our individual perception of society as fractured and fragmented on the one hand, and the 'real' state of affairs of social totality on the other.

> The concept of mediation has traditionally been the way in which dialectical philosophy and Marxism itself have formulated their vocation to break out of the specialized compartments of the (bourgeois) disciplines and to make connections among the seemingly disparate phenomena of social life generally.
>
> (*PU*: 40)

This might seem to be saying that a work of criticism (such as *The Political Unconscious*) can work as a *symbolic* 'unification' of the 'seemingly disparate phenomena' of life; but Jameson won't have this. The word he doesn't like in the previous sentence is 'symbolic'. The mediation of criticism like his is not symbolic at all. It is real, because the totality is real – which is to say, as a Marxist Jameson believes, that what he calls the 'seemingly disparate phenomena' of life are only *seemingly* disparate: in fact they are all expressions of an underlying totality. It is the fragmentation that is illusory.

> Such momentary reunification would remain purely symbolic...were it not understood that social life is in its fundamental reality one and indivisible, a seamless web, a single inconceivable and transindividual process, in which there is no need to invent ways of linking language events and social upheavals or economic contradictions because on that level they were never separate from one another.
>
> (*PU*: 40)

What Jameson sees himself as doing, in other words, is only making plain what is already the fact. A novel like *Mansfield Park* is already intimately connected to the realities of its social and economic environment; it only *appears* to be separate from them.

There's another level of mediation at work in Jameson's project here, though, and that is the mediation between the Hegelian and Althusserian viewpoints. It might seem that where a Hegelian would happily go along with Jameson's opinion that society is a totality (that art and economics are all part of the same whole), an Althusserian would surely disagree. For Althusser, the superstructure (for instance art) and base (economics) were 'semi-autonomous' from one another. But Jameson picks up on the 'semi' in that formulation: 'what must be said about the Althusserian conception of structure,' he insists, 'is that the notion of "semi-autonomy" necessarily has to relate as much as it separates. Otherwise the levels will simply become autonomous *tout court* [altogether], and break into the reified space of the bourgeois disciplines' (*PU*: 40–1). The point is that even Althusser believed that the economic base determined 'in the last instance' – that if you chased along the chain of connections far enough you would eventually come back to the economic facts of life. Jameson is able to mediate between Hegel and Althusser, to dialectically synthesise these apparently differing traditions. One crucial step he makes is to enlist Freud (or more particularly, Lacan) as a way of bridging the gap. He suggests that 'Totality' is like the Lacanian 'Real', which in turn suggests that, for Jameson, Marxist 'totality' is to be found in history rather than anything else. He argues that 'Lukacs' [Hegelian] conception of totality may here be said to rejoin the Althusserian notion of History or the Real as an "absent cause"'. Althusser is right to say that 'Totality is not available for representation, any more than it is accessible in the form of some ultimate truth' (*PU*: 54–5). But it is available, none the less, at second hand through various mediating forms, such as narrative (history 'is *not* a text...[but] history is inaccessible to us except in textual form' *PU*: 82). The difference becomes one of critical perspective: whether to write like Lukacs presupposing 'immanent or transcendent' unities which can be applied to the texts discussed, or whether like Althusser to concentrate on 'the rifts and discontinuities within the work' (*PU*: 56–7). Jameson thinks he can do both:

In the interpretive chapters of the following work, I have found it possible

> without any great inconsistency to respect both the methodological imperative
> implicit in the concept of totality or totalization, and the quite different atten-
> tion of a 'symptomal' analysis to discontinuities, rifts, actions at distance,
> within a merely apparently unified cultural text.

(PU: 56–7)

He is able to do this because these two fields concentrate on different parts of the text; this is what Freud/Lacan allows him to do. The rifts and discontinuities are present on the *surface* of the text (they are part of the *manifest* form of the text), in the same way that a psychiatric patient may exhibit dislocated and odd symptoms of neurosis. The total unity is present in the *unconscious* of the text (they are part of the *latent* form of the text), where literature inevitably refers back to and embodies the social and economic realities out of which it was created. For example – and this is a position Jameson elaborates at length in his Conrad chapter later in *The Political Unconscious* – the surface of Conrad's novels makes reference to a variety of dislocating and frag-menting particulars: a level of 'social reification', an idiosyncratic experimental writing style, and a sometimes wrenching use of narra-tive forms. But what these disruptions do is mark the place in the text where unconscious anxieties are buried, anxieties that are related to the shift in *socio-economic* realities from industrial to post-industrial capitalism (from realism to modernism), which is part of the larger totality of society and history.

Narrative, then, is for Jameson a key mode of mediating between the individual and society, as well as between the apparent fragmenta-tion of society and the real totality underlying it. Narrative might be the storyline of a Balzac novel, or it might be the critic Northrop Frye's narrative about the literary category of 'romance', which tells a sort of story about the development of a literary form over time. The advantage in narrative, Jameson argues, and the reason he focuses on that in particular in literary studies is that it provides comprehensive-ness without reducing the elements of the text to static or idealised elements. A story will link together all the protagonists, events, descriptions, and other textual elements, and, as such, narrative is the place in fiction most directly to express the 'unconscious' totality (or linked-togetherness) of real life. This is the meaning of the book's subtitle, 'Narrative as a Socially Symbolic Act'; the narratives that mediate our existences (from the myths and stories we tell ourselves, to the plot-lines of soap operas and novels) symbolically embody our social reality. This is why in the subsequent chapters of his book Jameson goes on to examine 'Romance', Balzac, Gissing and Conrad from the point of view of narrative practice.

MAGICAL NARRATIVES: ROMANCE AND EPIC

After the sometimes rather hard-core theorising of the first chapter 'on Interpretation', Jameson's second chapter starts to bring the critical project of *The Political Unconscious* to bear on more specific examples. 'Magical Narratives: On the Dialectical Use of Genre Criticism' explores the way Jameson's particular perspective on literature might be applied to the genres, with the fantastic adventure mode of 'the Romance' as his key example.

ROMANCE

The term is derived from the fact that the first medieval romances were 'in the Roman language' (Latin); 'Romance' has subsequently become a much broader literary or generic category. The first romances were popular courtly tales about the wonderful and sometimes far-fetched adventures of great chivalrous heroes such as King Arthur, Charlemagne or Alexander the Great. The storylines often involved magic, with heroes battling dragons to save damsels, travelling to exotic locations by strange means, and so on; they concerned battle, falling in love and usually ended happily. Early verse romances gave way in the fifteenth and sixteenth century to prose romances. The form was revived by writers like Walter Scott at the turn of the nineteenth century, whose interest in medieval romances shaped his own novels (it was the revival of interest in romance at this time that led to the early nineteenth-century being called the Romantic period). Throughout the nineteenth and twentieth centuries aspects of the romance form have been evident in children's literature, science fiction and fantasy, magic realism and many others.

Jameson chooses Romance from all the genres he might have chosen because, as he says at the chapter's beginning, Marx's own 'story' or 'narrative' of history as a whole (a story where the put-upon working people of the world struggle against their oppressors and eventually triumph living – literally – happily ever after) suggests a 'story with a happy ending' paradigm. This is to say that Marxism exists within the narrative framework of 'comedy' or 'romance' rather than (say) tragedy. As Jameson says, 'the Marxian vision of history' has been described by some 'as a "comic" archetype or a "romance" paradigm' (*PU*: 103). Jameson imagines a far future individual, living in communist utopia, looking back on the literature of our present tradition as 'monuments of power societies' works that inscribe oppression and violence as 'children's books recapitulating the barely comprehensible memory of ancient dangers' (*PU*: 103–4). It goes without saying, for Jameson at any rate, that this notional far-future literary critic will, in other words, be undertaken by a Jamesonian sort of reading of literature, focusing on what texts reveal about the socio-economics of our barbarous age and our even more barbarous past.

Marxist critics have often been primarily interested in so-called realist texts, because 'realism' was thought to be better suited to the business of revealing the actualities of life; but as Jameson points out the key nineteenth-century authors for the development of realism – he names the three novelists Walter Scott (1771–1832), Honore de Balzac (1799–1850) and Theodore Dreiser(1871–1945) – did not in fact write realism, as the term has since come to be understood; which is to say, they did not write quasi-scientific documentary novels drawn from research in the real world. Instead they drew on 'an exhilarating heterogeneity in their raw materials' and exploited 'a corresponding versatility in their narrative apparatus' (*PU*: 104). For instance, they mixed close observation of the world around them with some of the formal features of Romance. This point might seem arbitrary, but it is actually central to Jameson's approach. He is deliberately marking his critical perspective off from a narrowly conceived 'traditional' Marxism. To take an extreme example to make the point: for Stalin's regime, the only acceptable form of art was something called 'social realist' art – art which directly reflected the gritty oppressive realities of contemporary living, or else art which celebrated the triumph of proletarian strength in portraying an ideal communism. Works which were not 'realist' in *this* sense were likely to be condemned as 'escapist', as distracting ordinary people from the realities of their oppression in order to forestall revolution (to be seen, in other words, as 'false consciousness'). For Jameson this is to put too much emphasis on the *consciousness* of texts, on what they seem to be saying on the surface, and not enough on their *unconscious* – the ways in which, no matter how apparently escapist their surfaces, they still embody the social and economic realities that shaped them.

'The association of Marxism and romance therefore,' says Jameson, 'does not discredit the former so much as it explains the persistence and vitality of the latter' (*PU*: 105). That Romance remains vital seems hard to deny (the contemporary popularity of science fiction and magical realism, for instance, point to that), although non-Marxists are clearly going to have trouble with Jameson's implication that Romance flourishes because it embodies some essential Marxist truth. But Frye's opinion, quoted here by Jameson, that Romance is 'the ultimate source and paradigm of all storytelling' would be widely endorsed by many critics. Marxism, Jameson insists, is simply the most systematic and politically engaged version of that Romance impetus: politics with a happy ending.

DIACHRONIC VERSUS SYNCHRONIC

Accordingly, Romance makes a good starting place for Jameson to begin his interpretive work. He does this in two ways: by talking about the evolution of the romance form over time, and by comparing aspects of different romance texts to determine what 'romance' means in more general terms. The first, because it places a string of romances along a time-line one after the other, Jameson calls a 'diachronic' technique: 'chronic' means to do with time (as in 'chronometer'); the 'dia-' prefix means that there are various elements arranged across time. The second approach, because it ignores the changes over time but looks at all these romance texts at the same time to pick out similarities and differences, he calls 'synchronic' ('syn-' means together). These two organising principles, the diachronic and the synchronic, crop up repeatedly in Jameson's work. In a sense they dramatise the same argument between the particular and the total we looked at earlier under the rubric of 'Hegel versus Althusser'. Is 'romance' a series of more or less discontinuous individual texts all written at different times under different circumstances? (i.e. should we read it diachronically?) Or is it a total category, of which each individual romance is merely a partial expression? (i.e. is it more synchronic?). Faced with this dilemma, Jameson wants to have it both ways. He mediates the issue through narrative, in this case the narrative of the emerging romance form. This enables him to have his cake and eat it too, to see 'romance' as a total genre made up of all the romances that have been written and at the same time to focus on the particulars of individual examples of romance. It should be added that faced with a similar problem in looking at Adorno's writings (in *Late Marxism*), he opts straightforwardly for the synchronic: as he puts it 'as though the various Adornos in the various stages of their youth and decay (as in *2001*) were all sitting round a table in the British museum together' (*LM*: 3).

In this chapter Jameson's discussion of Romance is in the closest engagement with the work of the American critic Northrop Frye, whose influential *Anatomy of Criticism* describes a number of key archetypal story-patterns and characters. Romance for Frye is 'a wish-fulfilment or Utopian fantasy' (as, Jameson could add, is Marxism), in which 'a process of transforming ordinary reality' is undertaken (*PU*: 110). Frye's analysis is diachronic: he puts together a time-line of Romances, from medieval *romanciers* like Chretien de Troyes through Shakespeare to Scott and Dickens, and even up to P G Wodehouse. Then he draws out the parallels and continuities between these texts to isolate an evolving 'romance' archetype – a particular romance world, a hero ('analagous,' says Frye 'to the mythical Messiah or deliverer who comes from the upper world'), a villain, and a series of narrative happenings structured around a number of binary oppositions (high/low, angel/demon, white magic/black magic, spring/winter). Jameson has several interesting things to say about Frye's analysis. For instance, he notes the way it is predicated on the 'displacement of romance from some primary register in religious myth all the way to its degraded versions in the irony of a fallen world' (*PU*, 112–13). As a Marxist Jameson is unlikely to see this notion that Romance texts embody a degraded form of a 'pure' religious myth as anything other than a mystifying piece of 'bad' ideology, that reflects some deeper anxiety in the political unconscious. As he says, 'Frye has here projected the later categories of religion – the ideology of centralized and heiratic power societies – back onto myth, which is rather the discourse of decentred, magic-oriented, tribal society formations' (*PU*: 113); society comes first, of course. More crucially, for Jameson, Frye's particular ahistoricism – his ignoring of the specifics of historical context – misrepresents the genre fundamentally. To talk about 'character' for instance in the archetypal romance is to import a concept that, whilst being a commonplace nowadays, does not map onto earlier perceptions of the universe. These romance narratives derive in the first instance 'from a social world in which the psychological subject has not yet been constituted as such, and therefore in which later categories of the subject, such as 'character', are not relevant' (*PU* 124). What is wrong with the concept of character from Jameson's point of view (although he doesn't say this in so many words) is that it is a function of a bourgeoise individualism. This means that for Jameson 'character' is an ideological construction dating roughly from the eighteenth century (drawing on precursor texts by Cervantes and Shakespeare) which is part of a hidden ideological project to 'naturalise' the operations of capitalism by presenting society as a collection of autonomous individuals ('characters') rather than seeing individuals as socially constructed figures. When we think of 'characters' our thinking has been invisibly shaped by these historical circumstances, and we cannot escape this. Pretending that all people in all historical periods have always thought of 'character' as the same sort of thing is nothing but a form of mystification.

Shifted into the realm of literary criticism, Jameson implies that this deeply embedded piece of mystification simply doesn't account for texts very well. He gives an example: the 'character' of Heathcliff in Emily Bronte's *Wuthering Heights*. Criticism which tries to analyse the 'character' of Heathcliff works poorly ('romantic hero or tyrannical villain?' (*PU*: 126)) because he operates in ways so far removed from conventional notion of character. Heathcliff remains an enigma for this sort of criticism because it is looking for the wrong things: Heathcliff is not 'representational' of a human being (you will never meet an individual like him walking down your street), he is instead 'an impersonal process' the focus for disruptive forces that operate in the novel. As Jameson puts it:

> Heathcliff is the locus of *history* in this romance: his mysterious fortune marks him as a protocapitalist, in some other place absent from the narrative which then recodes the new economic energies as sexual passion. The ageing of Heathcliff then constitutes the narrative mechanism whereby the alien dynamism of capitalism is reconciled with the immemorial (and cyclical) time of the agricultural life of a country squiredom.
>
> (*PU*: 128)

In other words, a reading of *Wuthering Heights* needs to look at the socio-economic forces that shaped its composition: in this case the economic dynamic of the early nineteenth century, when industrial and trading capitalism was rising and replacing (disrupting) the older land-based agricultural order. Capitalism, Jameson follows Marx in conceding, *is* dynamic, it does get things done; but it also disregards human feelings, rides roughshod over people's needs and is otherwise brutal and oppressive. It is energetic and attractive, but also fundamentally dark, cruel and violent. In other words, capitalism is a Heathcliff figure. It is worth putting the equation round this way (rather than saying that 'Heathcliff is a "capitalism" figure'), because Jameson is very specifically *not* arguing that *Wuthering Heights* is an allegory of socio-historical circumstances. It is not that Emily Bronte set out to write a coded criticism of the rise of capitalism or that the job of the critic is to decode the novel. It is that all the literary resources available to her as a writer – the novel and romance modes she uses, the literary antecedents she alludes to and her own social and cultural determinants – already embodied, as a sort of unconscious, the socio-economic circumstances of her day. It is not, in other words, that Heathcliff is an allegorical version of 'capitalism' (in the way that Christian in Bunyan's *Pilgrim's Progress* is a straightforward coding of nonconformist Christianity). It is rather that 'capitalism' determines and conditions the way a 'character' like Heathcliff can be written in the first place.

Jameson's reading of Frye, then, is that although he pretends to construct a diachronic reading of Romance, in fact his 'micronarrative' (his little history of the genre) is not diachronic at all but synchronic, because it ignores the historical circumstances of each particular romance. Jameson himself puts together a diachronic account of Romance in this chapter, and he addresses the issue that he is doing exactly what Frye claims to be doing. He tells 'a historical narrative about the destinies of romance as a form' and concedes that 'it will be said that such a narrative (what I have elsewhere called a "diachronic construct") is…no less "linear" than the historical continuities affirmed by Frye' (*PU*: 136). To write such a history, he suggests, is to write a kind of romance about romance:

> a narrative in which a recognizable protagonist – some 'full' romance form realized, say, in the *romans* of Chretien de Troyes – evolves into the elaborate

Italian and Spenserian poems and knows its brief moment on the stage in the twilight of Shakespearian spectacle before being revived in romanticism...[through] Scott and Emily Bronte, only to outlive itself in modern times...[as] fantasy.

(*PU*: 136)

Jameson is rightly suspicious of this kind of story. As an example he cites Frye's account of the 'eiron' figure, the side-kick or helper figure of the hero. Frye defines the eiron as 'the type entrusted with hatching the schemes which bring about the hero's victory' and instances Roman comedy in which this figure 'is always a tricky slave (*dolosus servus*)' and Renaissance comedy in which 'he becomes the scheming valet'. Frye goes on:

Through such intermediary nineteenth-century figures as [Dickens's] Micawber and the Touchwood of Scott's *St. Ronan's Well*...he evolves into the amateur detective of modern fiction. The Jeeves of P. G. Wodehouse is a more direct descendant.

(quoted in *PU*: 136–70)

For Jameson the evolutionary language Frye uses hides the fact that its diachronic narrative is actually crudely synchronic; that the point of Frye's 'micronarrative' is actually to fit all these types, from a wide variety of differing socio-economic contexts, into one organic unified scheme. Not then to trace the development of these different manifestations of a romance type through such instances of the Roman slave and Micawber, but to 'produce a new narrative component which may be defined as a Micawber-considered-as-a-*dolosus-servus*' (*PU*: 137).

CONTENT, FORM AND THE POLITICAL UNCONSCIOUS

Jameson's point as before, then, is that it is not just the *content* of literary works that articulates political points, it is the *form* in which the content finds shape and expression. That the fact that a text belongs to a particular genre or genres (Romance, say, or novel) is as ideologically significant as what the characters get up to or whether it reflects the harsh realities of urban living. 'Genre is essentially a socio-symbolic message, or in other terms...form is immanently and intrinsically an ideology in its own right' (*PU*: 141). A critic needs to be aware of the ways in which the substance *and* the form of a given text relate to their socio-economic determinants, to the historical circumstances that shaped them in the first place. The critic also needs to notice the ways in which deviations in the form or content reflect anxieties in the political unconscious. Jameson gives the instance from the history of music, where 'folk dances are transformed into aristocratic forms like the minuet' (*PU*: 141). We could cite a more recent example: blues guitar music originates from a particular cultural context, specifically the poverty and class (and race) oppression of America's Deep South in the early years of the century. Nowadays it is one of the most lucrative of cultural forms in the world, its most famous practitioners multi-million-aires. There may be little difference in form and content between the early and the more recent blues; The Rolling Stones or Eric Clapton play a version of the same twelve-bar guitar form, and they still sing about being miserable, and a Frye-style criticism might insist that these later versions of the Blues exist in a synchronic, organic relationship to the work of Robert Johnson or Howlin' Wolf. But a Jamesonian approach would insist that a proper critical appreciation of 'the Blues' would need to be sensitive to the socio-economic facts of specific instances, and would see elements of both form *and* subject as expressive of differing political determinants. To elaborate a little, this would mean going beyond the vulgar Marxist observation that (oppressed black) Johnson sung about going to the crossroads and selling his soul to the devil whilst (affluent white) J.J. Cale sang about taking cocaine. It would mean examining the ways in which a form originally dominated by formal features like a self-conscious roughness of technique and repetition of structure, a form in which repressed political realities returned as tales of drunken lovelorn misery, adapted itself to the logic of late capitalism by becoming reified, concentrating on melody and expert musicianship, and shifting its focus towards a depthless elaboration of sex and consumption. In other words, the *formal* ways in which the Blues of the Rolling Stones deviate from the Blues of Robert Johnson is as revealing as the continuities; and form and content must be taken together.

Jameson closes his chapter on Romance with a 'base-superstruc-ture' diagram that sums up what he has been arguing, where the 'base' is the *substance* of literature, the history and ideology out of which it is constructed, and the 'superstructure' is the *form* the literature adopts – for instance, a 'novel in the Romance tradition' like *Wuthering Heights*.

FORM	*expression*	the narrative structure of a genre
	content	the semantic 'meaning' of a given mode
SUBSTANCE	*expression*	ideologemes, narrative paradigms
	form	social and historical raw material

An 'ideologeme' (under the bar) is a sort of ideological atom, the smallest unit into which ideological discourse can be broken by analysis – the individual pieces, as it were, of ideology. What this diagram does is give some sense of the subtle interactions of base and superstructural elements when applied to literary and cultural analysis. We might take as an example the mode of *epic* that Jameson mentions in passing here (*PU*: 146). Any given epic project, for example, Tennyson's attempt to write a national British epic in the nineteenth century in his *Idylls of the King,* needs to be examined in terms of the mutual determinations of content and form, although each of these will also affect the other. In the case of Tennyson, his choice of form was, if anything, more ideologically significant than his choice of content. Epic was intimately associated with expansionist patriotic celebration – with the golden age of Greece for Homer, Virgil with Imperial Rome, Dante with the splendour of medieval Italy, Camoens with the colonising voyages of Renaissance Portugal, and so on. Epic was seen as a national mode, and Tennyson (and many other nineteenth-century British poets) felt the need to write a national poem that reflected the new British empire, a large-scale ideological celebration of British nationhood. The key British epic before Tennyson was Milton's *Paradise Lost*, in which national ambition had been translated into religious expression. Tennyson opted to retell the mythic adventures of King Arthur in epic format, and the exercise which began as early as the 1830s was not completed until the 1880s – a period of composition that coincided with the expansion and consolidation of the British Empire. A Jamesonian reading of Tennyson's *Idylls* might argue that we can see how the *substance* of the poems uses the story of Arthur conquering Britain and imposing a particular patriarchal military code of 'order' upon it as a means of *expressing* the socio-political *content* of nineteenth-century British national life that Tennyson seeks to celebrate. Similarly, the choice of epic *form* involves a certain ideological *content* (a heroic poetic celebration of national adventure), which in turn expresses the narrative specifics of the text. This is where Tennyson's epic project gets particularly interesting; in fact, because in place of the more usual epic unity of narrative, *Idylls of the King* reads as unusually fragmented, a series of romance stories that are stitched together with varying degrees of consistency. It would be a fascinating undertaking to produce a critical reading of Tennyson's poem that read its formal breakage and fragmentation, together with its obsessive, or even neurotic, inflection of Arthurian myth as being about sexual betrayal and punishment, as reflecting precisely the anxieties and contradictions of nineteenth-century imperialism and bourgeois individualism. In the Jameson schema, the 'social and historical raw material' (which, in Althusserian phrase, are always the final determinant in the last instance) include within themselves the inequality, social fragmentation and individual alienation of high capitalism. Accordingly, these factors are going to determine both the expression of the substance – the way Tennyson's story becomes about the decline of Arthur's kingdom as much as its rise and the emphasis on the way Arthur's wife Guinevere cannot be controlled, such that her sexual infidelity destroys everything – and the larger arena of the form (the fragmented narrative structure, the irony and impossibility of 'straight' epic in a post-Romantic age). This is not a simple 'base determines superstructure' model, but a more Althusserian patterning, a more complex sense of the interrelations of all these ideological features. All these factors, determined ultimately though they be by the social base, exist nonetheless in a series of complex interrelations. As Jameson observes, 'each method, as it moves from the "form" of a text to the latter's relationship to "substance", completes itself with the complementary term' (*PU*: 147).

BALZAC, GISSING, CONRAD

The remaining three chapters of *The Political Unconscious* provide detailed readings of three classic nineteenth-century novelists by way of working through the implications of this theory in more practical terms. I will not summarise the ins and outs of these closer readings of texts as they depend, in the first instance, on a certain knowledge of the novels being discussed, and because they are easy enough to follow once the underlying critical principles have been grasped. But there is some merit in mentioning one or two of the points Jameson draws out of his analysis.

BALZAC AND THE UTOPIA OF THE HOUSEHOLD

Chapter 3, 'Realism and Desire', treats Honore de Balzac
(1799–1850), the French novelist who is particularly associated with
the development of realism. His *Comedie Humaine* (*The Human Comedy*)
is a series of ninety-one interlinked novels that draw on a rich wealth
of specific details drawn from Balzac's observation of the France in
which he lived during his lifetime. Balzac's novels – Jameson focuses
particularly on *La Vieille Fille* (*The Old Girl*) – provide a powerful sense
of an almost documentary verisimilitude, an illusion of actual lived
experience, against the background of which his various characters live
out their lives. Jameson is particularly interested in the way the omnis-
cient narrator of Balzac's novels, and that same detailed description of
the things of everyday life that provide the 'realist' texture, reflect the
increasing commodification of nineteenth-century capitalism. Jameson
quotes a passage from *La Vieille Fille* in which the well-to-do environs of
the novel are lovingly described ('On the balustrade of the terrace,
imagine great blue and white pots filled with wallflowers...[and]
homely vistas offered by the other bank, its quaint houses, the trickling
water of the Brillante...What peace! What calm!' (*PU*: 155) and argues
that 'in such an evocation...the desire for a particular object is at one
and the same time allegorical of all desire in general', *PU*: 156). This
sort of writing can be seen as characteristic of Balzac's 'realism', the
deployment of various details drawn from observation of life in
nineteenth-century France. Jameson, though, suggests that the particular choice and arrangement of these details creates not a sense of
verisimilitude, but a sort of literary special-effect, a bourgeois fantasy
whereby affluent living is presented as 'natural'. In Jameson's terms,
this 'utopia of the household' is the fantasy of the novel, the attempt to
escape from the 'tensions or inconsistency' of the actual world Balzac
purports to represent. That there is something obviously missing from
this particular fantasy (the realities of suffering, all the people excluded
by capitalism from enjoying the pleasant balustrade with its lovely
views) finds expression in the formal gaps of Balzac's novel: in the fact,
for instance, that *La Vieille Fille* is 'a narrative without a hero (in the
sense of a privileged 'point of view' or centred subject)' (*PU*, 169).
More particularly, the novel reflects the 'historical specificity of
Balzac's "moment"', a moment which existed 'before the full constitu-
tion of the bourgeois subject and the omnipresent effects of massive

reification – in which desire, the decentering of the subject, and a kind of open history are still conjoined' (*PU*: 169–70). A later realist like Gissing (treated in the following chapter) was unable to inhabit the fantasy of desire that Balzac puts at the centre of *La Vieille Fille*, because by the end of the century the logic of the socio-economic underpinning had changed.

Jameson ends his Balzac chapter with a more particularly Lacanian reading of another novel, *La Rabouilleuse*, in which he identifies Balzac's urge to paint the world as a bourgeois fantasy, his 'wish-fulfilling texts' as symptoms of the fact that they belong to the logic of the Lacanian Imaginary (see pp. 65). The implausible so-called 'realist' fantasies of these two novels are in fact versions of 'the fantasy of ultimate reinstatement in the mother's eyes…the first stage or moment in the process whereby the original fantasm seeks an (impossible) resolution' (*PU*: 181). As we might expect, this undermines Balzac's status as a 'realist' in Jameson's eyes:

> This moment – the production of the wish-fulfilling text – is not yet…the moment of genuine literary or cultural production, let alone of 'realism' in any sense this word can have. What it allows us to account for is the production of that quite different thing called ideology, which Althusser defines as 'the imaginary representation of the subject's relationship to his or her real conditions of existence'.
>
> (*PU*: 181)

In the case of Balzac, Jameson suggests, this 'imaginary relationship' included 'Balzac's vision of himself as a great Tory landlord' with 'local authority but also national influence…an ideological spokesman for the aristocratic elite'. It is this ideological ground that determines the particular shape of the 'fantasy' in Balzac's novels.

Finally, Jameson distinguishes between texts rooted in the logic of the Imaginary (like Balzac), with texts that, like the Lacanian subject, have entered into the realm of the Symbolic. 'Unlike the more degraded, and easily commodifiable, texts of the Imaginary level, these new second-level narratives…entertain a far more difficult and implacable conception of the fully realised fantasy' (*PU*: 183). The Lacanian 'Real' is, as Jameson has said elsewhere, History itself; it is the Real of History that provides 'unanswerable resistance' to Balzac's fantasy. When compared with historical narrative we realise how inadequate Balzac's imaginary narratives are. It is history on which Balzac's desires 'must come to grief'. More than that, the Real/History is, in our 'fallen world of capitalism', necessarily 'that which resists desire, that bedrock against which the desiring subject knows the break-up of hope and can finally measure everything that refuses its fulfilment.'

GISSING AND IDEOLOGICAL NARRATIVE

In Chapter 4 of *The Political Unconscious* Jameson reads George Gissing (1857–1903), the 'most "French", it has been said, of British natural-ists' (*PU*: 186). Like Balzac, Gissing wrote into his novels a great deal of closely observed 'realist' detail about, for instance, life in the slums of London. But Jameson, thinks that a novel like Gissing's *The Nether World*, is best read

> not for its documentary information on the conditions of Victorian slum life, but as testimony about the narrative paradigms that organize middle-class fantasies about those slums and about 'solutions' that might resolve, manage, or repress the evident class anxieties aroused by the existence of an industrial working class and an urban lumpen-proletariat.
>
> (*PU*: 186)

The key, again, is narrative, and in particular the way Gissing adapts and modifies two familiar narrative forms (especially associated with Dickens): one where a philanthropist changes the fortunes of down-at-luck characters with the proper application of generously donated money, another where happiness is found in what Jameson calls 'the idyllic space of family and child-bride as a Utopian refuge from the nightmare of social class' (*PU*: 188). These two narrative forms (Jameson implies) are so removed from reality as to constitute Imaginary (in the Lacanian sense) responses to the problems of social class. Gissing, writing in his particular historical period, no longer has access to them. His is a more 'symbolic' response. In his novel *The Nether World* both these narrative paradigms are invoked, and both are distorted or poisoned. On the one hand, the sweet, innocent character Jane does not find her happy marriage (more brutally, the other key female character, the haughty and beautiful working-class girl Clara, who leaves to become an actress, has acid thrown in her face). On the other, the philanthropic ambitions of Old Snowdon lead to nothing but misery, with his money eventually being stolen completely. Jameson is in no doubt that these 'ideologemes…drive home the same ultimate message for the lower classes: stay in your place!' (*PU*: 189).

CONRAD: ROMANCE AND WORK

Chapter 5, 'Romance and Reification', reads Conrad's novels, and *Lord Jim* in particular, as narrative constructions that register the shift from 'realism' (which in turn reflects or embodies nineteenth-century industrial capitalist economics) to 'modernism' (which is the early twentieth-century embodiment of a different economic logic). This chapter is unusually rich and detailed, and resists easy summary here. Baldly, it picks out the uses Conrad made of the 'romance' narrative paradigm (the adventure story); they way he, for instance, registers the sea as both an exciting arena for romantic adventure *and* simultaneously as a place of work. This is important to Jameson's purposes because it demonstrates how 'romance' and 'adventure', on the one hand, and the sorts of 'work' associated with the rise of capitalism in the eighteenth-century on the other, are actually part of the same ideological patterning. We might think of romance as the exact opposite of the dull day-to-day of ordinary work, but Jameson reads Conrad's novels in ways that reveal how both 'romance' and our contemporary sense of 'work' derive from the same historical and ideological determinants. Jameson also reads Conrad's distinctive (some might say notorious) written style as another formal embodiment of the social and economic shifts between the nineteenth century and the modernist period. A non-native speaker of English, Conrad's style is often idiosyncratic; it is always grammatical, but it sometimes produces lengthy, ornate sentences and peculiar idioms. Jameson suggests that Conrad's distinctive writing style looks forward to the stylistic experiments of modernism, where poets and novelists deliberately strained and warped the language to achieve particular effects. *The Political Unconscious* is not a book that examines the literary phenomenon of modernism, but the Conrad chapter ends with a nod in that direction:

> After the peculiar heterogeneity of the moment of Conrad [i.e. the fact that he is both realist and modernist], a high modernism is set in place which it is not the object of this book to consider. The perfected poetic apparatus of high

modernism represses history just as successfully as the perfected narrative apparatus of high realism did the random heterogeneity of the as yet uncentred subject. At this point, however, the political, no longer visible in the high modernist texts, any more than in the everyday world of appearance of bourgeois life, and relentlessly driven underground by accumulated reification, has at last become a genuine Unconscious.

(*PU*: 280)

SUMMARY

The Political Unconscious is an attempt to redefine the grounds of criticism, and to suggest the ways a critic needs to be like a Freudian analyst in looking beyond the 'surface' or obvious elements of a book or poem. This is one reason why the book has had such a profound impact on the world of literary criticism: it encourages critics to rethink their own positions, and it comes up with a new definition of what 'interpretation' involves. To quote Satya P. Mohanty, *The Political Unconscious* demonstrates that 'textual meaning is not simply discovered; it is *produced* in a mediated way. Interpretation is, for Jameson...an opening up of the text to the winds of history' (Mohanty 1997: 99–100). The most influential aspects of Jameson's rich and suggestive critical undertaking have been:

- The usefulness of Freudian, psychoanalytical categories, and particularly that of the *unconscious*, to the business of Marxist criticism.
- The role of *history* as the ultimate shaping force on any text.
- The fact that narrative is the key *mediational* category in contemporary society, with the consequence that the novel has become the most important mode of literature.
- A powerful account of *Romance* and its connections with the history and ideology of the eighteenth and nineteenth century.

5

MODERNISM AND UTOPIA

Fables of Aggression

The Political Unconscious (1981) was mostly concerned with nineteenth-century literary forms such as 'realism'. Jameson is also particularly well known for his analyses of the late twentieth-century cultural forms known as 'postmodernism', which are dealt with in the following chapter. This chapter seeks to link these two categories, by looking at the various work Jameson has done on the literary period between the nineteenth and the later twentieth centuries, the movement known as modernism that flourished particularly in the early years of this century. It focuses in part on *Fables of Aggression* (1979), his study of the modernist Wyndham Lewis (1882–1957), but it is also a chapter that seeks to draw together some of the major points of Jameson's work up to the early 1980s.

The major contexts for Jameson's thought – his ubiquitous Marxism, drawing as much from Lukacs and Adorno as from Althusser and others, and his engagement with Freud and more particularly Lacan – do need to be grasped if we are to understand his concept of 'the political unconscious'. A number of central concepts appear and reappear in Jameson's work:

- A constant return to 'history' as the key to understanding and working with texts, such as but not exclusively literary works; for

Jameson history is the Lacanian Real, always approached but which absolutely resists symbolisation.

- A fascination with issues of 'interpretation' as an open-ended and inevitable mediation of experience.
- Linked with this last, a belief that texts embody *repressed* features of historical anxiety and trauma, and that a critic needs to focus on the pathological 'neuroses' of writing and culture as a clue to the buried 'unconscious' of literature.
- A linked concern with *reification*.
- An insistence on looking at the *form* (style, genre, etc.) of a literary work in addition to, or even in preference to, its apparent *content* (story, character, and so on). The particular form that Jameson is most interested in is *narrative*.
- A strong commitment to the *dialectical* process, to what Jameson calls 'stereoscopic thinking'.

In the chapters on Jameson and the Marxist traditions (Chapters 1 and 2) I talked about the various aspects of a particular fault-line running through Marxist theory today, with the Hegelian Marxists on one side and the 'Althusserian' or relativist Marxists on the other. Jameson's own orientation towards a sort of Hegelian 'totality' seems to position him on one side of this debate, but as I have argued in fact his position is more dialectical than that. Indeed, this is a good place to state what has probably become apparent here in the chapters leading up to this one. Jameson is particularly interested in three 'movements' of Western literature and culture: nineteenth-century 'realism', early twentieth-century 'modernism' and late twentieth-century 'postmodernism'. In each case, he is drawn primarily to novelists (he rarely writes about poetry or drama, although his later work has dealt extensively with cinema), and in each case he sees the aesthetic criteria as manifestations of more basic social and economic – historical – ones. In other words, he does not see the broad shifts in cultural practice from realism to modernism to postmodernism as just a feature of literature; he sees it as being very precisely tied in with *historical* changes in the structures of capitalism out of which 'realist' and 'modernist' writing gets produced. This is made particularly plain in his chapter on Conrad in *The Political Unconscious*, because Jameson regards Conrad as a writer on the cusp between realism and modernism. So, 'realism' (multiform though that literary mode was) embodies the artistic response to the nineteenth-century consolidation of Capitalism as the dominant social form, at least in Western civilisation. He argues that modernism reflects a shift in the emphasis of Capitalism in the West (one connected with such things as the massive industrialised conflict of World War I) to a more thoroughly industrialised, fragmented and alienating system. Following on from this, as I discuss in the following chapter, postmodernism is not merely a sort of artistic 'school', not a 'style' that includes certain features (surface rather than depth, fragmentation, etc.), but is itself what the subtitle to Jameson's *Postmodernism* book calls it – 'the Cultural Logic of Late Capitalism'. For the division of Capitalism into early, middle and late phases Jameson relies on the sociological and history studies of sociological thinkers like Weber and Mandel, and accordingly he takes these terms from conventional literary studies – 'realism', 'modernism' and 'postmodernism' – as more like shorthand terms for a matrix of socially and historically determined artistic phenomena.

'Realism' has already been discussed (see pp. 83). It is worth spending a little time here on 'modernism', partly because it is a term that becomes increasingly important as Jameson examines its successor, 'postmodernism', and partly because it is part of the task of *Fables of Aggression* to analyse the movement of which Wyndham Lewis was a part.

MODERNISM

This term is used by various critics in various ways to refer to a body of literature produced mostly in the first half of the twentieth-century; most critics think that it has now been superseded by postmodernism, although there are some who argue that modernist literary practices continue vigorously today. Authors generally classified as modernist have often very different styles; from the novels of Joseph Conrad (1857–1924) and D.H. Lawrence (1885–1930) to the more experimental prose of Virginia Woolf (1882–1941) and Dorothy Richardson (1873–1957); the poetry of T.S. Eliot (1888–1965) and Ezra Pound (1885–1972), or the drama of Bertolt Brecht (1898–1956). What all these writers share is a fascination with literary experiment, with making a 'new' literature that was deliberately unlike the 'realist' art of Victorian culture. Modernist literature is often startling and challenging; it may, for example, be written in a fractured or peculiar style, or it may advocate the overturning of traditional values. David Forgacs identifies in modernism the following features: 'first, it is, or was, about novelty; it was a set of artistic practices which shared a commitment to "make it new" in Pound's phrase...many modernist artists envisaged political change in terms of a radical and often violent break...it has been argued that modernism was an art of "depth" not of "surfaces"' (Forgacs 1995: 9–10). One of the things that is significant for Jameson's purposes is that the most famous 'modernist' works were being produced during the 1930s, at a time when Adolf Hitler was coming to power in Germany, and Benito Mussolini in Italy – a time, in other words, when fascist political systems were in the ascendant. Jameson is interested in the interconnections between this political history and the artistic practices of modernists themselves.

Jameson's subtitle to the *Fables of Aggression* book in a sense gives the game away: *Wyndham Lewis, the modernist as Fascist*. Lewis (1882–1957) is perhaps an unlikely figure for a committed Marxist like Jameson to want to spend a whole book discussing. An avant-garde experimental writer of tremendous power and inventiveness, whose novels – in particular *Tarr* (1918) and *The Apes of God* (1930) – have won him many admirers, he was nonetheless a deeply unpleasant man. He attacked his contemporaries, and much of the age in general, with a searing satirical vituperation, and believed that the solution to what he saw as the degeneracy of the times was to be found in fascism. His admiration for Hitler, and even more for Mussolini, was heartfelt and deeply unpleasant. He was also a thoroughgoing misogynist, whose sexism and hatred of women manifests itself frequently in his writings.

Clearly, this explicit fascism and sexism constitutes a position with which a Marxist like Jameson will have little or no sympathy, and it would be possible – or even easy – merely to dismiss Lewis as a fascist and leave it at that (John Carey does this in his study of modernism, *The Intellectuals and the Masses*). But Jameson's response is not so crude. He finds the fascism and the sexism unpalatable, but he also recognises the fierce beauty of much of Lewis's writing. It is not that the 'good' features of Lewis's work can be separated out from the 'bad' – very specifically, according to Jameson, they cannot. It is that precisely the 'bad' elements (I put these terms in inverted commas because Jameson repeatedly expresses disdain for the 'good guys and bad guys' simplicity of such judgmental criticism) function as manifestations of *latent* issues that are central to 'modernism'. In some ways Lewis is a typical modernist, in others he is atypical: he shares, for instance, the emphasis on stylistic and formal experimentalism with James Joyce, but he does not share Joyce's 'monadism', his treatment of characters as if they possessed psychological individuality, something after the manner of nineteenth-century realists (*FA*, 14). Jameson argues that it is in the way that Lewis breaks with modernism, rather than the ways in which he is a representative modernist, that are most 'positive', most useful. The vehemence and anger of Lewis's work, of which his beguilement by the violence of fascism and his hatred of women are two manifestations, is key. Lewis 'expresses the rage and frustration of the fragmented subject at the chains that implacably bind it to its other and its mirror image' (*FA*: 61). In other words it is the ways in which Lewis's novels are about rupture, about breaking with conformism, that make them valuable.

Here is an example of Lewis's style, from his most famous novel *Tarr* (1918). The character Kreisler is in his apartment, looking down on Paris in more than one sense.

> Kreisler was shaving himself, one eye fixed upon Paris. It beat upon this wall of Paris drearily...The late spring sunshine flooded, like a burst tepid star, the pink boulevard: beneath, the black-suited burgesses of Paris crawled like wounded insects hither and thither...Imagining yourself in some primitive necropolis, the portraits of the deceased covering the holes in which they had respectively been thrust, you would, pursuing your fancy, have seen in Kreisler a devout recluse who had taken up his quarters in this rock-hewn death-house.
>
> (Lewis 1918: 69)

According to Jameson, Lewis's style works as the 'registering apparatus for forces which he means to record, beyond any whitewashing and liberal revisionism, in all their primal ugliness' (*FA*: 21). Other modernists to one degree or another smoothed over the ugliness of 'modernist' existence, the reification and alienation, the consequences of the First World War; Lewis did not. The saving grace, as far as Jameson is concerned, is that this stylistic, formal resistance, this repudiation and rupture, is so powerful that it even disrupts what Lewis presumably did not mean it to disrupt – his fascist masculinist *content*.

Lewis did not fully know what he was doing: he wanted to write novels that put across a fascist message. But Jameson's 'political unconscious' style of reading is able to read against the grain, to find Marxist value in these otherwise easy-to-dismiss modernist works. Lewis would have hated it, but that is not the point.

Presumably (he doesn't actually say as much), Jameson chose to produce a study of Wyndham Lewis because, in part, he represents the most extreme, the most fascistic and unpleasant, of all the modernists. In other words, he is setting out to show that a properly dialectical criticism cannot be distracted by only the manifest content of literature; it needs to seek out the socially significant *latent* content too. This must always be brought back to history ('always historicize!'), so that any critical reading of modernism that ignored the historical circumstances out of which that literature was produced — in particular the aftermath of the First World War and the rise of Fascism and Nazism across Europe — will always fall short.

JAMESON AND MODERNISM

Jameson's own position on modernism represents 'a critique and synthesis all at once' of what he considers to be 'the two great rival theories of modernism current today' (*FA*: 13). This is, it should be noted, a slightly idiosyncratic perspective on the myriad different angles of what is, today, the much-contested term 'modernism'. The contemporary critic Peter Nicholls has argued that, far from being a monolithic cultural phenomenon, modernism is 'a highly complex set of cultural developments at the beginning of the twentieth century' (Nicholls, vii). Nonetheless, Jameson positions himself in the middle of a binary, the pro-modernists and the anti-modernists.

> On the one side,' he says, 'we inevitably confront [Marxist critic Georg] Lukacs' apologia for nineteenth-century realism, in which modernism is denounced as the symptom and reflex of late capitalist social relations. On the other, equally predictably, we find ranged in order the various ideologists of the modern itself, all the way from the great Anglo-American and Russian modernists to Adorno and the Tel Quel group: for them the formal innovations of modernism are to be understood as essentially revolutionary acts, and in particular the repudiation of the values of a business society and of its characteristic representational categories.
>
> (*FA*: 13)

In other words, characteristic features of modernist writing – a self-proclaimedly new and avant-garde approach, stylistic experimentation, writing that strives not to be mistaken as 'realist', an elite aesthetic that prizes difficulty and erudition and so on – can be read either way. Lukacs disliked this constellation of 'modernist' attributes because they (he thought) enshrined everything that was wrong with capitalist industrialised society as aesthetic values: they made alienation and fragmentation into virtues instead of recognising them as social and ideological ills. Alternatively, it is possible, as Jameson notes, to see these features as attempts to disrupt and break apart the stifling conformism and reification of the modernist age.

The key name on Jameson's list, as we might expect, is Adorno; and as we have already seen in discussing this influential figure (pp. 6, 41) a vital concept is that of resistance. If we take it for granted that the realities of society are hidden from us by ideological sleight-of-hand, then it can be argued that one of the most important things a work of art can do is shake us up, challenge our assumptions, encourage us to take nothing for granted. For Adorno, the masterpieces of modernist art achieved this revolutionary ideal with their difficult style and experimental approach to subject, and above all with their repudiation of the nineteenth-century modes of realist writing that pretended to show the world as it really is, but in fact merely reproduced the dominant ideology of domesticity and property.

Jameson can see merits in both the pro- and anti- camps. He bridges the gap between them by suggesting that they are both partly right. The key for him is *reification*. More specifically, the operations of capitalism in the early twentieth-century resulted in 'a fragmentation of the psyche and of its world' that opened up 'the semi-autonomous and henceforth compartmentalized spaces of' differing modes of being in the world ('lived time' versus 'clock time; for instance; the rhythms of the body as against the stricter rhythms of the machine) (*FA*: 13). What he means by this is that one of the consequences of capitalism coming to dominate society is that the more organic 'rhythms of the body' become squashed into the artificial time-slots required by the system, such that we are compelled to get up when we are still tired to go to work, to eat when we are not hungry because that is when lunch-hour is time-tabled, and so on. The machine-logic that breaks life into segments, into separate compartments, became increasingly prevalent as the twentieth century proceeded, and is reflected in its art and literature. The point is that modernist fascination with fragmentation of form and style 'not only reflects and reinforces such fragmentation and commodification of the psyche as its basic precondition', but at the same time 'the various modernisms all seek to overcome that reification as well by the exploration of a new Utopian and libidinal experience of the various sealed realms or psychic compartments to which they are condemned' (*FA*: 14).

In *The Political Unconscious* Jameson analysed portions of Conrad's writing in these terms, finding evidence for Conrad's early-modernist 'Utopian vocation' in 'extreme moments of intensity' (*PU*: 230) such as a passage describing a storm in Conrad's story *Typhoon* (1903). Here is the passage from Conrad:

> At its setting the sun had a diminished diameter and an expiring brown, rayless glow, as if millions of centuries elapsing since the morning had brought it near its end. A dense bank of cloud became visible to the northward; it had a sinister dark olive tint, and lay low and motionless upon the sea, resembling a solid obstacle in the path of the ship. She went floundering towards it like an exhausted creature driven to its death…The far-off blackness ahead of the ship was like another night seen through the starry night of the earth – the starless night of the immensities beyond the created universe, revealed in its appalling stillness through a low fissure in the glittering sphere of which the earth is kernel.
>
> (Quoted in *PU*: 230)

According to Jameson 'such passages virtually fashion a new space and a new perspective, a new sense of depth, out of sheer color' (*PU*: 231). He goes on, in a good example of the Jamesonian 'difficult' style I talked about in the Why Jameson? section:

> The operative presence of motifs from the late nineteenth-century positivist or Wellsian metaphysic of entropy (the diminished sun, the approaching end of the universe, the night of the cosmos beyond the night of the earth) is nonideological insofar as the conventional relationship between narrative and ideology is here reversed. In such 'purer' descriptive passages, the function of the literary representation is not to underscore and perpetuate an ideological system; rather, the latter is cited to authorize and reinforce a new representational space. This reversal then draws ideology inside out like a glove, awakening an alien space beyond it, founding a new and strange heaven and earth upon its inverted lining.
>
> (*PU*: 231)

We see all the elements of Jameson's own style here: the profusion of polysyllabic words, the subordinate clauses, the complex shifts of thought from an allusion to the science fictional writing of H.G. Wells (1866–1946) through questions of ideology and representation to the metaphor of the glove. What Jameson is saying here is that Conrad draws on the sorts of images and literary techniques we might associate with the apocalyptic imagined futures of an author such as Wells. He classifies an author like Wells as belonging to the 'positivist' nineteenth-century tradition; positivism was a philosophical school that turned away from spiritual and abstract issues and believed that science was enough in itself to comprehend the universe. Jameson implies that Wells's dismal prophetic visions of the world ending in 'entropy' – winding-down and fading out – embodies a straightforward ideological belief that the decadent world of the late nineteenth-century was exhausted and rundown. But he goes on to argue that Conrad's modernist revision of these tropes 'reverses' this ideological coding. The Utopian intensity of Conrad's writing operates here in style and form rather than content, up-ending conventional ideological attitudes, turning the metaphorical 'glove' inside out and showing us something completely new.

> The ideological allegory of the ship as the civilized world on its way to some doom is subverted by the unfamiliar sensorium, which, like some new planet in the night sky, suggests senses and forms of libidinal gratification as unimaginable to us as the possession of additional senses, or the presence of non-earthly colors in the spectrum.
>
> (*PU*: 231)

'Sensorium' is Jameson's phrase to describe Conrad's manner of aesthetically rendering sensual experience (the experience of the senses); and 'libidinal gratification' or the gratifying of the libido is a Freudian allusion to the pleasures human beings can experience. What Jameson is saying here, in other words, is that Conrad's style undoes what might otherwise be the conventional effect of a story about a ship sailing through a storm, in which the ship would be taken as an allegory for civilisation and the storm would be the forces threatening to destroy it (this, Jameson implies, is what an H.G. Wells story about a ship in a storm would imply). In place of this, and in keeping with the stylistic experiments of modernist writing, Conrad allows us to think in new ways about the way our senses perceive things, and about the pleasures that gives us; that instead of 'realist' allegory he writes a modernist Utopia.

This emphasis on the Utopian aspect of modernist writing – the way so many modernist writers (novelists like James Joyce, Wyndham Lewis, or poets such as William Butler Yeats, Ezra Pound and Laura Riding amongst many) want to withdraw from the unpleasantness of the world around it into a better, more cultured Utopian space – also touches on one of the most enduring of Jamcson's fascinations: Utopia.

JAMESON AND UTOPIA

Jameson's writings return over and again to the notion of Utopia; indeed according to the contemporary critic Philip Goldstein, this Utopia transcendentalism – which is to say, this attempt to 'transcend' or go beyond the problems of present-day living into Utopian possibilities – is one of the most characteristic things about Jameson's writings. A commitment to 'Utopia' explains why, for instance, Jameson is always coming back to analyses of science fiction, that mode of writing in which the everyday is most obviously 'gone beyond'. But even his readings of mainstream writers attempt to 'find utopian ideals' in sometimes unpromising material, as with Lewis, above, and throughout his work Jameson is in 'pursuit of a utopian realm transcending "instrumental" institutional conflicts' (Goldstein 1990: 149, 151). In this respect Jameson is following a Marcusean reading of Marx. Marx himself distrusted the Utopian impulse: he thought, in Jameson's words, that 'Utopian thought represented a diversion of revolutionary energy into idle wish-fulfillments and imaginary satisfactions' (M&F: 110–11). Marx repeatedly stressed the need for *practical* thought as a foundation for revolutionary resistance to the system of capitalism. But Marcuse believed, and Jameson agrees, that times have changed: 'now it is practical thinking which everywhere stands as a testimony to the power of that system to transform even its adversaries into its own mirror image. The Utopian idea, on the contrary, keeps alive the possibility of a world qualitatively distinct from this one.' (M&F: 111).

UTOPIA

This phrase was coined by Sir Thomas More, the sixteenth-century writer, thinker and politician. He wrote a book in Latin, the scholarly language of his day, about an imaginary country in which everybody was contented and the people all lived in harmony with one another. The name of this country was a learned pun (in Greek 'eu-topia' means 'good place', and 'ou-topia' means 'no place', which reflects the fact that More's country was both non-existent and a portrait of ideal good). The word is now used to describe any conceptual country or place where the evils of present-day living have been eradicated. Any country with perfect social and political system is likely to be called a Utopia.

Utopia has been a perennial theme of human discourse. Philosophers and political thinkers have pondered how we might convert our flawed world into a Utopia; and Karl Marx is only one of the most widely influential of these theorists. Many world religions have promised Utopias: Christianity, for example talks of a second coming of its Messiah, an event which will be followed by the setting up of a perfect society on the Earth for a thousand years. And literature and culture has demonstrated a repeated fascination with the ideas of Utopia that no critic can afford to ignore. Thomas More's original book of *Utopia* was one kind of text in this respect: a rational, scholarly anatomy of a possible perfect society. But there are many other forms of Utopian literature, from the rhapsodic poetry of the last act of Percy Bysshe Shelley's visionary *Prometheus Unbound* (1819) to the science fiction future of the long-running TV series *Star Trek*.

If we conceive of Marxist 'communism' as a form of Utopia, then it is difficult to be too precise about exactly how it might actually operate. Marx's own pronouncements are a little vague (he gives us only hints such as 'from each according to their abilities, to each according to their needs'), and the most we can say is that we can at least be sure that a Marxist Utopia was *not* realised in Stalin's Russia. Jameson, in fact, argues that disillusionment with the communist experiment produced in the 1950s a waning of interest in Utopianism, but that there was a 'reawakenng of the Utopian impulse' in the 1960s, something that found its manifestation in wide-ranging cultural optimism apparent as much in the 1968 student protests and flower power as in a new acceptance for fantasy such as J.R.R. Tolkien's *The Lord of the Rings* (1954–5) or Ursula LeGuin's novel *The Dispossessed* (1974). Jameson's essay 'Of Islands and Trenches: Neutralization and the Production of Utopian Discourse' (in *IT2*) invokes 'islands' and 'trenches' in its title because, as he observes, Thomas More's original land was separated from the mainland by having a trench dug around it transforming it into an island. For Jameson what this signifies is not just that Utopia is a place removed from the world we all live in (indeed, that a Utopia like Thomas More's is actually a deliberate *negation* of all the features of More's England, a sort of anti-real world). We might expect that, but Jameson's point is more subtle, that the Utopian imagination has often worked by a process of exclusion and pushing away. In other words, Utopias have often not solved the problems of society but just expelled them outside their boundaries. Of More's Utopia he notes that 'many of the unpleasant tasks associated with the market and commercial activity' are simply pushed 'outside the city walls'. Money, for instance, 'is excluded, and then used exclusively in foreign trade'. Another example is war, removed from More's perfect world by the expedience of hiring foreign mercenaries to fight Utopia's battles for it. In other words, that two of the most problematic features of the actual world – money and violence – are not 'solved' but instead 'ejected and then re-established outside the charmed circle that confirms the Utopian commonwealth' (*IT2*: 100). This 'act of disjunction/exclusion' that Jameson argues 'founds Utopia as a genre' is where its problems begin; because this disjunction and repression is itself an act of violence.

It is worth dwelling on this point for a moment, because it goes to the core of Jameson's thinking about Utopia and therefore his whole political programme. For Jameson, the danger with Utopian thinking is that it assumes a uniformity, a conformity: it has often been imagined as a place where everybody is happy *in the same way*, where people miraculously fit harmoniously with other people because nobody sticks awkwardly out from the whole. But as Jameson observes, people only 'work' socially because they have been taught to repress antisocial impulses, and a world in which everybody had been utterly purged of antisocial thoughts would be a world completely defined by repression. As we might expect, Jameson equates repression with violence, and this results in an interesting paradox. This is because Jameson argues that Adorno defines Utopia as *the world free of violence* ('the mark of violence, whose absence, if that were possible or even conceivable, would at once constitute Utopia' (*LM*: 102). So, in place of the monolithic conformist Utopias in the Thomas More tradition (with their magical avoidance of the damaging repression their fantasies require), Jameson postulates something more diverse, something that shares features with what we shall soon define as postmodernism:

a Utopia of misfits and oddballs, in which the constraints for uniformization and conformity have been removed, and human beings grow wild like plants in a state of nature: not the beings of Thomas More, in whom sociality has been implanted by way of the miracle of the utopian text, but rather those of the opening of Altman's *Popeye*, who, no longer fettered by the constraints of a now oppressive sociality, blossom into the neurotics, compulsives, obsessives, paranoids, and schizophrenics whom our society considers sick but who, in a world of true freedom, may make up the flora and fauna of 'human nature' itself.

(*LM*: 102)

It is not coincidental that Jameson reaches for an example from contemporary popular culture to illustrate his idea of Utopia. The celebration of diversity and the particular instead of totality and uniformity is one of the key features of postmodernism, and for Jameson as we shall see postmodernism is something particularly connected to popular culture. It might seem trivial, but in this Jameson is following on from Adorno himself, whose version of Utopia is that of a person on a lilo floating on the water and basking in the sunshine, the Utopia of '*rien faire comme une bête* [doing nothing like an animal], lying on water and looking peacefully at the sky' (*Minima Moralia*: 208/157).

Adorno himself, it should be said, would not thank Jameson for this popular culture citation; as we have seen, Adorno launched potent attacks on what he called 'the Culture Industry', devoted as it is to churning out deadening hypnotic popular culture in the form of films, music and latterly TV, all of which has the effect of distracting ordinary people from the social injustices under which they (we) live, of turning us all into non-political non-revolutionary sheep. But Jameson thinks that postmodernism has changed the way popular culture works. In *Late Marxism* he wonders 'whether watching thirty-five hours a week of technically expert and elegant television can be argued to be more deeply gratifying than watching thirty-five hours a week of 1950s "Culture Industry" programming.' He goes on:

> The deeper utopian content of postmodern television takes on a somewhat different meaning, one would think, in an age of universal depoliticization; while even the concept of the Utopian itself – as a political version of the Unconscious – continues to confront the theoretical problem of what repression might mean in such context.

(*LM*: 142–3)

We have already looked at the ways in which Jameson took over the Freudian notion of the Unconscious and applied it to social and political contexts. Here we have another definition of precisely what 'the political unconscious' actually is: Jameson thinks of it as the Utopian impulse, which is in itself repressed by the social superego – we see why repression is so incompatible with Jameson's ideas of Utopia. At the same time, Jameson is tentatively suggesting that the fractured, decentred, surface-fixated variety of postmodern television can in its own way embody Utopia.

This moves us on to the cultural phenomenon of postmodernism, which occupies the next chapter. It is important to bear in mind, however, the ways in which Jameson's most recent criticism does not represent a break or departure from earlier work.

SUMMARY

The features touched on in this chapter have included:

- The way Jameson is able to read a writer at the opposite political extreme to himself, such as Wyndham Lewis, in ways that reveal valuable insights.
- An account of *modernism* that sees it as a literary and cultural response to the reification of contemporary life.
- The importance of *Utopia* and Utopian thinking in Jameson's thought.

6

POSTMODERNISM, OR
THE CULTURAL LOGIC
OF LATE CAPITALISM

Jameson's engagements with the cultural phenomenon of 'postmodernism' began to appear in the early 1980s. An article entitled 'Postmodernism and consumer society' was published in a collection of essays in 1983; this essay, considerably revised, appeared as 'Postmodernism, or the Cultural Logic of Late Capitalism' in the British journal *New Left Review* in 1984. It is this article that has been more often cited and probably more discussed than anything else Jameson has written. Douglas Kellner has called it 'probably the most quoted, discussed, and debated article' of the 1980s, and Hans Bertens describes it as having been 'immensely productive and...seminal in getting the more traditional, that is non-poststructuralist, left involved in the discussion' about postmodernism (Bertens 1995: 160). This article then appeared in book form as the first chapter of Jameson's enormous 1991 book, *Postmodernism, or The Cultural Logic of Late Capitalism*. This chapter is going to examine this famous statement on the boundaries and logic of postmodern culture, partly with a view to positioning it in the discourses surrounding postmodernism out of which it grew, and partly to try and explain just why it has been so influential. But the first thing to note is the way in which Jameson's approach to the postmodern condition has always been thoroughly Marxist. Where previous theorists had looked at postmodern poetry, or art, or architecture, as a style or a series of styles, Jameson was the first to link it directly to socio-political circumstances – to history, in other words. Just as realism was an embodiment, in terms of literary form, of nineteenth-century capitalism, and modernism was the expression of the reified, post-industrial capitalism of the early twentieth century, so what postmodernism is (for Jameson) is the expression on an aesthetic and textual level of the dynamic of 'late capitalism'. Clearly, late capitalism has a particular economic logic, one which is different in various ways from the old capitalisms of the nineteenth century (fewer workers have old-style factory jobs, for instance; more are working in service industries; less emphasis is placed on manufacturing actual things like tables and cars, more on knowledge and the exchange of knowledge with TV and the Internet). Just as capitalism has this economic logic, so it also has a cultural logic, and the cultural logic of late capitalism is what we call 'postmodernism'.

DEFINING THE POSTMODERN

It is very hard to define the term 'postmodernism' straightforwardly, partly because it is a complex phenomenon and partly because different critics refer, as we shall see, to different versions of it. At the most basic level, the word 'postmodern' suggests a period that comes after the modern. To begin with this was the sense in which word was used, a recognition that the aesthetic project of modernism, which had seemed so vital in the early years of the century, had become dissipated. A new dominant in culture had been emerging since World War II, and had achieved a high profile in the 1970s. As Jameson himself (among many) has argued, modernism had emerged as a self-conscious reaction against nineteenth-century realism, with writers trying deliberately to 'make it new' and overturn what they saw as the outmoded artistic principles of realism. We saw in the chapter on *The Political Unconscious* that Jameson's reading saw the difference between realism and modernism to be, in fact, the expression of different economic logics; his account of Conrad sees that novelist as straddling this divide, caught between, on the one hand, the economics of work and (factory) production that is behind 'realism', and, on the other, the newer, more reified and international capitalisms of the early twentieth century (modernism).

Modernism constitutes an enormous and powerful body of writing and art, and some critics – even, as we shall see, some critics closely associated with postmodernism – refuse to accept that it has passed away. Jameson, however, is unambiguous in pointing to 'the waning or extinction' of 'the hundred-year-old modern modern movement', or more specifically to the 'ideological or aesthetic repudiation' of modernism, as the place of birth of the postmodern. (*P*: 1). Before we come to exactly what Jameson argues in his ground-breaking 1984 essay, it will help to contextualise him with a look at three critics who went before him in the arena of debate over this term.

IHAB HASSAN

The first is Ihab Hassan, the first critic of stature to put forward the label 'postmodernism' as a description of contemporary artistic practices. In 1971 he published an article called 'POSTmodernISM: a Practical Bibliography'; later the same year he followed this up with a book, *The Dismemberment of Orpheus: Toward a Postmodern Literature*. Hassan's aesthetic sympathies were with modernist art, particularly the literature of minimalism and focused negation associated with writers like Franz Kafka and Samuel Beckett and composers like John Cage. He recognised a difference in the literature of the 1960s and 1970s, but at the same time it is not clear from Hassan's writing in what ways this 'new' literature differs from the 'old' modernism of the pre-war years. In *The Dismemberment of Orpheus* Hassan labels this new writing 'postmodern', but also insists that this term does not describe a new *period* in literature, but rather a particular *sort* of literature that has been present in Western culture for several hundred years, lurking in the background as it were. In particular, modernism contained within it, as a sort of more extreme version of itself, the thing that Hassan calls postmodernism: 'the postmodern spirit lies coiled within the great corpus of modernism...it is not really a matter of chronology: Sade, Jarry, Breton, Kafka acknowledge this spirit' (Hassan 1971: 139). Postmodernism involves resistance, negation, the spirit of 'unmaking' that Hassan calls the 'literature of silence'. Actually, modernism is also concerned with this for Hassan, but postmodernism is more self-reflexive and ironic about this project, more indeterminate and sometimes more playful. What this means is that critics following Hassan need not limit their studies of postmodernism to works published in the later third of the twentieth century; they can write (and some have) studies of 'postmodern modernism', 'postmodern Renaissance drama', and the like. The important thing is to recognise the hallmarks of a postmodern style, a postmodern approach to the limits and purpose of art. In an appendix added to *The Dismemberment of Orpheus* in 1982, Hassan usefully lists those features, opposing them with the features that he thinks define modernism – although, again, many of the terms in the right hand column of this famous list can be seen as more extreme versions or strategically dialectical oppositions of the terms in the left, and modernism is not actually separated from postmodernism so acutely.

Modernism	*Postmodernism*
Romanticism/Symbolism	Pataphysics/Dadaism
Form (conjunctive/closed)	Antiform (disjunctive, open)
Purpose	Play
Design	Chance
Hierarchy	Anarchy
Mastery/Logos	Exhaustion/Silence
Art Object/Finished Work	Process/Performance/Happening
Distance	Participation
Creation/Totalization	Decreation/Deconstruction
Synthesis	Antithesis
Presence	Absence
Centring	Dispersal
Genre/Boundary	Text/Intertext
Paradigm	Syntagm
Hypotaxis	Parataxis
Metaphor	Metonymy
Selection	Combination
Root/Depth	Rhizome/Surface
Interpretation/Reading	Against Interpretation/Misreading
Signified	Signifier
Lisible (Readerly)	*Scriptible* (Writerly)
Narrative/*Grande Histoire*	Antinarrative/*Petite Histoire*
Master	Code Idiolect
Symptom	Desire
Genital/Phallic	Polymorphous/Androgynous
Paranoia	Schizophrenia
Origin/Cause	Difference-*Différance*/Trace

Metaphysics	Irony
Determinacy	Indeterminacy
Transcendence	Immanence

It would take too long to explain all the terms in this list; but several of them draw on concepts introduced into the debate during the 1970s by other critics. Hassan's complex and sometimes contradictory attitude to his hybrid modernism–postmodernism rather muddies the business of definition, but one obvious point is the radical difference between his position and that of Jameson. Hassan is careful to separate out post-modernism from politics and economics; Jameson sees postmodern-ism as precisely the articulation on the cultural level of those forces. Hassan sees postmodernism as a 'style' as manifest in the writings of eighteenth-century libertine and pornographer de Sade, as in the novels of Kafka or Thomas Pynchon. For Jameson, the writings of de Sade and Kafka refer to a different political unconscious than that of contemporary novelist Pynchon. Jameson sees Hassan's 'postmodern' delight in play and indeterminacy as actually a form of 'deconstruc-tion', an attempt to deal with 'the postmodern aesthetic in terms of a more properly poststructuralist thematics' (*CT*: 22). What this means is that although Hassan says that he is talking about 'postmodernism', Jameson thinks he is actually talking about the techniques of decon-struction.

JEAN-FRANÇOIS LYOTARD

Perhaps even more influential than Hassan's work has been a short book by Jean-François Lyotard called *The Postmodern Condition* (1979). Asked to produce a 'report on knowledge' by the Quebec provincial government, Lyotard surveyed an enormous range of disciplines, particularly in the sciences and social sciences. Jameson wrote the introduction to the English translation of this little book, in which he describes it as a sort of 'crossroads' in which the various debates on the term were staged.

Lyotard's key insight has become one of the most influential short hand definitions of 'the postmodern': the overturning or erosion of master narratives. Like Jameson (although there is probably little direct influence between the two), Lyotard sees the stories people tell them-selves and one another as crucial. More than this, he sees certain of these stories – Christianity, for instance, or the story of the 'progress' of science and rationality – are 'metanarratives' – stories about stories that shape people's sense of themselves in the world. For a devout Christian, for instance, the whole world and the whole of history is part of one grand narrative, the working out of God's plan: everything fits into this story, everything has its place. The same is true of the Enlightenment project of rationality, which enabled people to believe that science and reason would make the world an increasingly better place in which to live. But, said Lyotard, what postmodernism represents is the breaking down of these 'master narratives'. It is no longer possible to believe in a grand story that explains everything. From the various relativisms and uncertainties of scientific discourse, Lyotard extrapolates out into a general indeterminacy, a suspicion of metanarratives. This is a position close to the attitudes of deconstructionists, of course, and is clearly opposed to Jameson's position. For Jameson, as we saw in the chapter on *The Political Unconscious*, literature and culture only made sense if placed in the context of a grand narrative – Marxism. Faced with the diversity of theme and subject of Greek tragedy, Renaissance poetry, nineteenth-century fiction and modern literature – all in many ways very different from one another – a critic needs recourse to a larger pattern:

> Only Marxism can give us an adequate sense of the essential *mystery* of the cultural past...These matters can recover their urgency for us only if they are retold within the unity of a single great collective story...[the story of] Marxism, the collective struggle to wrest a realm of Freedom from a realm of Necessity; only if they are grasped as vital episodes in a single vast unfinished plot.
>
> (*PU*: 19–20)

But Lyotard reserved a special hostility for Marxism, which he identified squarely with the practical Communism he despised as an agent of massive human misery. There is a certain gleefulness in which he tolls the death knell of one of the most potent of 'master narratives'. In fact we can argue, as Perry Anderson does, that it was actually 'just one "master narrative"' that lay at the core of Lyotard's animus.

> Marxism. Fortunately, its ascendancy was now at last eroded by the innumerable little tidings from the Gulag [i.e. tales of misery from communist regimes].

> It was true that in the West there existed a grand narrative of capital too; but it was preferable to that of the Party, since it was 'godless' – 'capitalism has no respect for any one story', for 'its narrative is about everything and nothing'.
>
> (Anderson 1998: 29)

Clearly, again, there are crucial differences between this position and anything that might be advanced by a critic such as Jameson.

JURGEN HABERMAS

The third critic whose name is often associated with postmodernism is Jurgen Habermas, a highly-respected German philosopher of left-wing sympathies. Habermas has spent much of his career constructing a model of ethical rationality, that is, of determining how liberal democracy ought to be run according to principles of disinterested reason and justice that create a consensus without forcing difference and minorities into an oppressive conformity. He thinks highly of what he calls 'the project of modernity', the culmination of Enlightenment attempts to order human affairs rationally. In earlier ages science, morality and art were seen as merely components of a larger whole (which Habermas calls 'revealed religion'); the Enlightenment separated out these realms and did away with the confusion (the bad science, the oppressive morality, the limited art) that resulted from blurring them together. Now science, morality and art could be judged not according to 'religious correctness' but according to newer, better categories of 'truth', 'justice' and 'beauty', respectively. But this laudable project had not yet been realised; modernity was in Habermas's term 'an incomplete project'. This was because the separate realms had not been integrated into society, made available to everybody. Instead they had become elite and specialist arenas from which people were excluded. Habermas considers that the nineteenth century saw an increasing removal of art from real life, something that various modernist writers attempted to overturn with acts of avant-garde experimentalism. They had failed, Habermas thought, because all three realms – not just art, but morality and science as well – needed to be brought into the public realm together.

But Habermas sees postmodernism, with its distrust (or even outright hostility) of reason, its demolishing of the categories of 'truth', 'beauty', and even of morality, as a terrible backward step.

Habermas thinks that the chances of undoing this terrible disintegration 'are not very good. More or less everywhere in the entire Western world a climate has developed that furthers currents critical of cultural modernism' (quoted in Anderson 1998: 38). For Habermas, as Jameson notes 'the vice of postmodernism consists very centrally in its politically reactionary function' (*P*: 58). In other words, Habermas sees postmodernism as politically *conservative*; not something that many intellectuals associated with the phenomenon would find flattering (for all his aversion towards communism even Lyotard is hardly right-wing). In Anderson's words 'whatever the criticisms to be made' of the intellectual traditions Habermas attacks as postmodern 'it cannot by any stretch of the imagination be described as "conservative"' (Anderson 1998: 40). Jameson, as we might expect, thinks we can understand Habermas's position only in its historical socio-political context: 'we need to take into account the possibility that the national situation in which Habermas thinks and writes is rather different from our own', because 'the silencing of a left culture...has been on the whole a far more successful operation [in Germany] than elsewhere in the West' (*P*: 59).

Other influential debates concerning postmodernism have come out of the discipline of architecture – it was to describe a new post-war architectural style that the phrase 'postmodernism' was first coined. Jameson himself mentions the novelist Tom Wolfe's study of twentieth-century architecture *From Bauhaus to Our House* (even though it is largely 'undistinguished'). It is a book generally in favour of the newer architecture, even if it lacks any 'Utopian celebration of the postmodern'; but what chiefly characterises it is a 'passionate hatred' of modernist architecture, such that any newer architecture has got to be better than what has gone before. More generally appreciated is the work of critic Charles Jencks, whose *The Language of Post-modern Architecture* (1978) found much to celebrate in the new style. 'Modernism suffers from elitism' he argued, echoing a common critical perspective that modernist artists were deliberately obscure because they despised the uneducated masses and only valued the opinion of the social and intellectual elite. 'Post-modernism is trying to get over that elitism' with an enthusiastic and sometimes vulgar amalgamation of 'the commercial slang of the street'. This breaking down of the barriers between High Art and popular culture is one of the things that Jameson himself picks up in his own analyses of the postmodern.

THE POLITICS OF THEORY

Jameson published 'The Politics of Theory', an article examining these conflicting approaches to the question of postmodernity, in 1984; it later became Chapter 2 of the *Postmodernism* book (it is also, confusingly, reprinted in *The Cultural Turn*). Despite the fact that many of the names I have mentioned here (particularly Hassan and Lyotard) specifically separated out 'postmodernism' as a cultural happening from questions of politics, Jameson insists that 'the problem of postmodernism – how its fundamental characteristics are to be described...– this problem is at one and the same time an aesthetic and a political one'. He goes on to insist that 'the various positions that can logically be taken on it' are always, necessarily, 'visions of history in which the evaluation of the social moment in which we live today is the object of an essentially political affirmation or repudiation' (*P*: 55). To make his point clear, he arranges the key names in the debate in a grid (adding the little-known Venetian architecture historian Manfredo Tafuri, who attacks both modernist and postmodern architecture as oppressive and mystifying manifestations of capitalism):

	ANTI-MODERNIST	PRO-MODERNIST
PRO-POSTMODERNIST	Wolfe Jencks	Lyotard
ANTI-POSTMODERNIST	Tafuri	Habermas

The question which follows, I suppose, is where we would place Jameson on a grid such as this. But in an important way, Jameson's critique of 'postmodernity' goes beyond the sort of 'plus or minus' value judgements suggested by the thinkers named above. This is at the core of the way that Jameson's theorises postmodernity, and it helps to explain why his 1984 essay on the subject had the sort of impact it did. Because Jameson was really the first major critic to insist on seeing postmodernism as a manifestation of certain *political* and *historical* circumstances. Late capitalism, a phrase Jameson adopts from the economist Ernest Mandel, represents a new economic logic, the third phase of capitalism development that has gained ascendancy over the older capitalism forms sometime after World War II. It follows that there will be a new cultural logic. Indeed, as far as Jameson is concerned, 'post-modernism' is 'something like a literal translation' in cultural terms of the economic descriptor 'late-capitalist'.

> To say that my two terms, the *cultural* and the *economic* thereby collapse back into one another and say the same thing, in an eclipse of the distinction between base and superstructure that has itself often struck people as significantly characteristic of postmodernism in the first place, is also to suggest that the base, in the third stage of capitalism, generates it superstructures with a new kind of dynamic.
>
> (*P*: xxi)

In other words, we see here, characteristically, the traditional vocabulary of Marxism (where base straightforwardly determines superstructure) combined with a more Althusserian version (where the distinction between the two is much more problematic); which is what we have seen in Jameson's distinctive Marxism all along (see above p. 29).

But more to the point, there is little virtue in being 'for' or 'against' postmodernism, except in the very general sense in which a Marxist can be 'against' capitalism (the same capitalism that shaped realism and modernism). 'Postmodernism', as the cultural logic of late capitalism, *is*, it needs to be understood, analysed, demystified, not skittishly 'embraced' or tetchily 'condemned'.

> The point is that we are *within* the culture of postmodernism to the point where its facile repudiation is as impossible as any equally facile celebration of it is complacent and corrupt. Ideological judgement on postmodernism today necessarily implies...a judgement on ourselves as well as our artefacts.
>
> (*P*: 62)

'POSTMODERNISM AND CONSUMER SOCIETY'

The essay 'Postmodernism and Consumer Society' first appeared in 1983; it is reprinted (altered somewhat) in *The Cultural Turn*. The first thing we notice about it is how firmly Jameson — unlike Hassan or Lyotard — draws a distinction between 'modernism' and 'postmodernism'. Although modernism was 'formerly subversive', the situation now is that the great modernist poetry of Pound, Eliot or Wallace Stevens; the International Style [in architecture] (Le Courbusier, Gropius, Mies van der Rohe); Stravinsky; Joyce, Proust and Mann – felt to be scandalous or shocking by our grandparents are, for the generation which arrives at the gate in the 1960s felt to be the establishment and the enemy – dead, stifling, canonical, the reified monuments one has to destroy to do anything new.

(*CT*: 2)

By contrast, Jameson lists artists and architects who can be thought of as 'postmodern', as creating in reaction against the dead hand of modernism:

the poetry of John Ashberry...the reaction against modern architecture and in particular against the monumental buildings of the International Style; the pop buildings and decorated sheds celebrated by Robert Venturi in his manifesto *Learning from Las Vegas*; Andy Warhol, pop art and the more recent Photorealism; in music, the moment of John Cage but also the later synthesis of classical and 'popular' styles found in composers like Philip Glass and Terry Riley, and also punk and new wave rock with such groups as the Clash, Talking Heads and the Gang of Four; in film everything that comes out of Godard – contemporary vanguard film and video – as well as a whole new style of commercial or fiction films, which has its equivalent in contemporary novels, with the works of William Burroughs, Thomas Pynchon and Ishmael Reed on the one hand, and the French new novel on the other.

(*CT*: 1)

This, then, is 'postmodernism'; Jameson is not comfortable defining or categorising what all these individuals have in common – as he says in the 'Introduction' to *Postmodernism*, it is best 'not to systematize a usage' or 'impose any conveniently coherent thumbnail meaning' (*P*: xxii). The term, as we have seen, is highly contested; Jameson thinks it 'internally conflicted and contradictory' too, although he also thinks that 'we cannot *not* use it.' What all these different artists, from John Ashberry to the Talking Heads, have in common is that their art is the expression of a new logic of capitalism, a cultural logic. Beyond that, and the fact that all these people are in sharp reaction to modernism, the thing that strikes Jameson most about postmodernism is 'the erosion of the older distinction between high culture and so-called mass or popular culture' (*CT*: 2). This is not just reflecting the fact that

Philip Glass and post-punk pop music can appear in the same list: it is that 'postmodern' artists deliberately draw on both traditions – Glass himself, for instance, has scored and adapted tracks from David Bowie's *Low* album for orchestra in his own minimalist 'high art' idiom. It is this eruption of the popular into the realm of high art that, Jameson thinks, most upsets academics (read: Habermas or Hassan) who oppose the way postmodernism has developed.

> This is perhaps the most distressing development of all from an academic standpoint, which has traditionally had a vested interest in preserving a realm of high or elite culture against the surrounding environment of philistinism, of schlock and kitsch, of TV series and *Reader's Digest* culture...but many of the newer postmodernisms have been fascinated precisely by that whole landscape of advertising and motels, of the Las Vegas strip, of the Late Show and B-grade Hollywood film, of so-called paraliterature with its airport paperback categories of the gothic and the romance, the popular biography, the murder mystery and the science fiction or fantasy novel. They no longer 'quote' such 'texts' as a Joyce might have done, or a Mahler; they incorporate them, to the point where the line between high art and commercial forms seems increasingly difficult to draw.

(*CT*: 2)

Jameson goes on in 'Postmodernism and Consumer Society' to analyse exactly what this 'postmodernism' constitutes, stressing that for him 'it is not just another word for the description of a particular style', it is also 'a periodizing concept' which correlates to 'a new type of social life and a new economic order – what is often euphemistically called modernization, post-industrial or consumer society, the society of the media or the spectacle, or multinational capitalism' (*CT*: 3).

POSTMODERNISM, OR THE CULTURAL LOGIC OF LATE CAPITALISM

The original 'Postmodernism and Consumer Society' essay limited itself to describing 'only two of [postmodernism's] significant features' which Jameson called 'pastiche and schizophrenia' (*CT*: 3). With the enlargement of the essay to the piece that was published in *New Left Review* (and which is reprinted as the first chapter of *Postmodernism*) the analysis is considerably expanded, to dwell on 'the following constitutive features of the postmodern' (*P*: 6). Jameson sees as postmodern 'a new depthlessness, which finds its prolongation both in contemporary "theory" and in a whole new culture of the image or the simulacrum' as well as a 'weakening of historicity, both in our relationship to public History and in the new forms of our private temporality'. Postmodern culture exhibits 'a whole new type of emotional ground tone' (Jameson refers to this as 'intensities'). He also identifies 'the deep constitutive relationships of all this' as grounded in 'a whole new technology, which is itself a figure for a whole new economic world system'.

This is a lot to take on board of a sudden, but it can be described easily enough as an elaboration of these two categories 'schizophrenia' and 'pastiche'. In turn, these manifest a shift away from time and towards space as the dominant mode of structuring cultural experience: sight, the most distant of the senses, becomes 'supreme'.

SCHIZOPHRENIA

This term, which crops up frequently in discussions of the postmodern, does not invoke the traditional psychiatric-clinical definition, where schizophrenia is a distressing delusional state characterised by loss of internal relation with one's own mental process, such that thoughts and impulses are thought to derive from 'voices' or 'visions' external to the mind, with a resulting apathy, eccentricity and isolation. Jameson uses the phrase as a shorthand, via Lacan, to be specifically opposed to *paranoia*. Clinically, 'paranoid' individuals see the world around them as a giant conspiracy, centred on themselves – perhaps in the form of 'everybody is out to persecute me'. Lacan used the term in a more theoretical sense: as he puts it, in a manner of speaking, all of us are paranoid. Our only way of apprehending the universe around us is to construct an 'I', an ego, around which we orient all our knowledge. For some critics, the 'paranoid' model can be thought of as modernist: a text such as *Ulysses* follows the ordinary day of an ordinary Dubliner, but everything that happens in the novel is related to a secret grand design, whereby the ordinary Leopold Bloom is on another level the heroic Greek Odysseus. In place of this closed pattern, postmodernism can be thought of as an opening up, a breaking down of tied narratives. Instead of relating the ego to one grand narrative, the 'schizophrenic' in this mode opens him or herself to a multiplicity of inputs, all on the same level as the ego. Lacanian schizophrenia represents 'a break-down in the signifying chain' (*P*: 26). The term is particularly associated with the European theorists Deleuze and Guattari, whose *Anti-Oedipus* (1983) celebrates the potential of this schizophrenic model in characteristically florid terms:

> taking a stroll outdoors...he is in the mountains, amid falling snowflakes, with other gods or without any gods at all, without a family, without a father or a mother...everything is a machine. Celestial machines, the stars or rainbows in the sky, alpine machines – all of them connected to those of his body. The continual whirr of machines.

The point here is, as Jameson says, when schizophrenia 'becomes generalized as a cultural style' it loses the 'morbid content' it would possess as an individual pathology and 'becomes available for more joyous intensities' (*P*: 29).

The postmodern subject for Jameson, determined as ever by social circumstance, necessarily reflects the increasing reification and fragmentation of late capitalism. We witness, he says, 'the end of the bourgeois ego' in the sense of a unified ego-construction; in its place people's sense of their own subjectivity is much less centred or focused. Moreover this release from 'the centred subject' involves 'not merely a liberation from anxiety but a liberation from every other kind of feeling as well, since there is no longer a self present to do the feeling' (*P*: 15). This is a radical thesis indeed; not that people like you or I are incapable of feeling anything, but that there has more generally been what Jameson, in a famous phrase, calls a 'waning of the affect' (*P*: 10), a fading-away of emotional content. Postmodern art is characterised by irony and cynicism, by a modish detachment from feeling anything – because, Jameson thinks, we no longer have the sort of subject that is very good at feeling. This has many consequences: we regularly see movies, for instance, which are enormously violent, enormously sexually explicit, without finding ourselves much moved by either, although our grandparents' generation found much milder representations of these things quite unacceptable on the screen, or anywhere else. We are alienated, in a manner of speaking, from our own emotions too: it becomes impossible to say a phrase like 'I love you madly' with a straight face (this example derives from Umberto Eco); we need to fall back on distancing tactics that foreground our self-awareness, and say instead something like 'as Barbara Cartland would say, "I love you madly"'.

This 'schizophrenic' subject, then, leads us to Jameson's second concept: pastiche, 'the disappearance of the individual subject, along with its formal consequence...engender the well-nigh universal practice today of what might be called pastiche' (P: 16). 'Pastiche' is a sort of copying or appropriation of the forms and styles of other literature. It has a strong family resemblance to parody, where a satirist writes a version of a well-known work in order to make some point. For example, the English Romantic poet Felicia Hemans (1793–1835) wrote a famous poem called 'The Homes of England' which includes the quatrain:

> The stately homes of England,
> How beautiful they stand!
> Amidst their tall ancestral trees,
> O'er all the pleasant land.

This was parodied by English satirist Noel Coward in a 1938 song:

> The stately homes of England,
> How beautiful they stand,
> To prove the upper classes
> Have still the upper hand.

There is some point to this parody; Coward is – wittily – unearthing the relationships of power and class that are mystified by Hemans' rose-tinted poem. But according to Jameson, under postmodernism parody ceases to be a potent cultural force; it 'finds itself without a vocation' whilst 'that strange new thing pastiche slowly comes to take its place' (P: 17). Pastiche is parody emptied out of content: 'it is a neutral practice of mimicry, without any of parody's ulterior motives, amputated of the satiric impulse, devoid of laughter...pastiche is thus blank parody, a statue with blind eyeballs' (P, 17). We might choose an example from film, appropriately because Jameson sees cinema as one of the pre-eminent postmodern forms (because of its stress on the visual). Ridley Scott's 1981 film *Blade Runner* is often cited as a thoroughly representative postmodern text. As a film it simultaneously inhabits the visual idioms of a 'futuristic' science fiction, and a retro *film noir* that evokes the 1930s. The technology is forward-looking, the dress styles, dialogue and situation of a form of 'private detective' narrative is backward-looking. But Scott does not 'quote' these filmic styles of *noir* in order to make any specific point about that time or ours; it is rather a matter of surface styling. As another example, we might want to compare the actual, directed anger of 'punk rock' as manifested in an album such as the Sex Pistols' *Never Mind the Bollocks* with the postmodern directionless emotion of Nirvana's album *Nevermind* (an album whose very title seems a laconic, wearied shortening of the Pistols' original). Kurt Cobain layers the 'raging' of punk-influenced guitar noise underneath an ironically detatched vocal persona, 'ah well, whatever, never mind'. The Sex Pistols parodied British patriotism ('God Save the Queen, the Fascist Regime'), where Nirvana are all about pastiche.

DEPTHLESSNESS

In all this what Jameson is identifying is a certain emptying out of significance, a flattening that leads to what he calls 'depthlessness'. Where under previous cultural logics art has involved some emotional or intellectual *depth*, postmodern art is thrall to the 'waning of the affect'. In a pungent demonstration of the difference Jameson reprints two famous pieces of visual art: Vincent Van Gogh's painting 'A Pair of Boots' (1887), the vivid and painterly representation of two worn old brown boots of the sort that a nineteenth-century peasant might have worn. The visual texture of this work of art is rich and involving, the detail rendered boldly and sensually. Jameson contrasts this famous image with a screen print by Andy Warhol from the 1960s, 'Diamond Dust Shoes' (both these images are reproduced in *Postmodernism*). This is a cluttered conglomeration of women's smart shoes, seen from above and rendered in tones of grey. There is no illusion of depth here, no visual perspective and no markers of context or explanation. Jameson sees a highly significant breach between these two art works. The Van Gogh contains within it, in a manner of speaking, 'the whole missing object world which was once [the shoes'] lived context…the heavy tread of the peasant woman, the loneliness of the field path, the hut in the clearing, the worn and broken instruments of labor in the furrows and at the hearth' (*P*: 8). But the Warhol image is nothing like this; not so much empty as lacking even the space in which this sort of 'depth' could be conceived.

> Andy Warhol's *Diamond Dust Shoes* evidently no longer speaks to us with any of the immediacy of Van Gogh's footgear; indeed, I am tempted to say that it does not really speak to us at all. Nothing in this painting organizes even a minimal place for the viewer...We are witnessing the emergence of a new kind of flatness or depthlessness, a new kind of superficiality in the most literal sense, perhaps the supreme formal feature of all the postmodernisms.
>
> (*P*: 8–9)

For a critic like Jameson who has throughout his career been wedded, as we have seen, to one particular version of a surface–depth model – the Freudian–Marxist 'political unconscious' where the surface of the text refers to the hidden 'depth', the content of history – this represents the most striking development in postmodernism. In this current 'culture of the simulacrum' (*P*: 18) the very concept of the real has been thoroughly problematised.

SIMULACRUM

This word, which means an image, copy or shadowy likeness of something, derives from the writings of the ancient Greek philosopher Plato, who thought the whole world was simply the copy of a better, purer world that existed on some other level of being (which he called the world of Forms). Its currency in debates around postmodernism stem from an essay by the French critic and theorist Jean Baudrillard called 'The Precession of Simulacra' (1983). Baudrillard, another critic to emerge from the Marxist tradition, argues that Western capitalism has moved from being based on the production of things to the production of *images* of things, of copies of 'simulacra'. Today we live in a world where the difference between 'real life' and 'simulated life' (or 'simulacrum') has degraded to a point where it becomes hard to tell one from the other: a world where millions fight the Gulf War through their television screens – indeed where the war appears to us as if it were actually happening on television rather than in real life; where newspapers report the goings-on of soap opera characters as if they were real because people care more for the 'artificial' characters of soap operas than for their own neighbours. Baudrillard calls this state of affairs 'hyperreality', where reality and simulation are received as being no different from one another: his prime example is Disneyland, which (he argues) is neither real nor simulated, neither true nor false. The old model where the copy comes after the original is overturned, now the 'simulacrum' *precedes* the real, hence the title of Baudrillard's essay.

Jameson reads Baudrillard's 'simulacrum' chiefly in visual terms, following another French critic Guy Debord in diagnosing 'a society in [which] "the image has become the final form of commodity reification"' (*P*: 18). Predominantly visual, the culture of postmodernism ranges everything before the eye, giving it a *spatial* logic (on the TV or cinema screen, or the new-designed spaces of postmodern architecture) that undermines the *temporal* logic that had gone before – the logic of time as, for instance, history that has been so important to Jameson's critique in earlier works. As Jameson puts it:

> The new spatial logic of the simulacrum can now be expected to have a momentous effect on what used to be historical time. The past is hereby modified: what was once, in the historical novel as Lukacs defines it, the organic genealogy of the bourgeois collective project…has meanwhile itself become a vast collection of images, a multitudinous photographic simulacrum.
>
> (*P*: 18)

A nineteenth-century historical novelist like Walter Scott (analysed in detail by Lukacs) could access 'history' as a real thing, the organic continuous line that defined Scott and his class. But postmodern art cannot access history in this way; history becomes merely a set of styles, depthless ways of approaching the past 'through stylistic connotation, conveying "pastness" by the glossy qualities of the image and "1930s-ness" or "1950s-ness" by the attributes of fashion' (*P*: 19). We can see this in the *Blade Runner* example mentioned above, but it is true even in texts that purport to bring to life a historical period: in a film like *Titanic* the clothes and the *look* are appropriate to the historical period, but the characters and their motivation, the dialogue and whole dynamic of the film operate on the level of continuous 1970s–1990s present (so, Kate Winslet's character gives the 'fuck-you' finger gesture to her would-be fiancé, something quite inconceivable for a well-bred young woman in the actual early years of the century). Historical action films like *Robin Hood: Prince of Thieves* or *First Knight* know enough to realise that there were no handguns in medieval England, and so equip their characters with bows and crossbows instead: but these crossbows will still fire a seemingly endless supply of bolts *as if they were* guns loaded with ammunition. Historical accuracy is only on the surface.

This loss of history is something Jameson considers traumatic, but as we might expect this trauma is 'repressed'. There *is* still a 'depth' to society; history and society still determine culture (the very concept of 'the cultural logic of late capitalism' speaks to this), even though post-modernism denies this depth and flattens it out. But Jameson notes the way the way 'historicism', or the urge towards history, has become in a sense 'neurotic'. He identifies a current fascination with 'nostalgia', particularly in film.

> Nostalgia films restructure the whole issue of pastiche and project it onto a collective and social level, where the desperate attempt to appropriate a missing past is now refracted through the iron law of fashion change and the emergent ideology of the generation.
>
> (*P*: 19)

Like the character in the TV series *Quantum Leap*, who is condemned to leap about in history, but only the history of his own lifetime, and so visits the historical periods of the 1950s, 1960s, 1970s and 1980s over and over again, this depthless postmodern historicity is focused above all on the instant nostalgia for the immediate past. Jameson identifies George Lucas's *American Graffiti* (1973), a film that recreates the style and look of 1950s America in loving detail, as 'the inaugural film of this new aesthetic discourse', the nostalgia film. Nowadays a decade like the 1950s is chiefly accessible to us as a series of particular *styles*, as a certain fashion in clothing, as a musical sound, and so on, rather than as an actual historical period. People may inhabit this 'style' if they like, but it does not involve them apprehending any actual historical consciousness. Indeed, one definition of 'postmodern' style is that it permits the mix-and-match of clothing and music from each of the stylistically significant decades of the twentieth century, the 1950s, the 1960s, the 1970s and the 1980s (we might, perhaps, want to add the '1930s' to this list, as a glance back to a pre-war 'distant' past).

Everywhere Jameson looks under the logic of postmodernism he sees much the same thing. 'The latest generation of starring actors continues to assure the conventional functions of stardom (most notably sexuality) but in the utter absence of "personality"' (*P*: 20). The older generation of actors like Marlon Brando or Laurence Olivier were genuinely sexy, or could actually act: the postmodern screen star projects a blank pastiche of this older 'style'. Pop music like that of the Beatles and the Rolling Stones is 'high-modernist' (*P*: 1) compared to the postmodern emptying out and simulation of Oasis or Primal Scream. In each case there is a slightly different genealogy to be traced out, the shift from 'modernist' to 'postmodernist' happens at a slightly different time – presumably (although Jameson nowhere actually spells this out) depending on how long it takes the underlying economic reality of 'Late Capitalism', which begins in the late 1940s, to filter up to the cultural level.

If all this sounds as if Jameson is charting a vulgar decline from former greatness, it needs to be stressed that this is not what is happening. It is important to hold on to Jameson's disinterested assessment of the phenomenon of 'postmodernism', beyond a simple 'good' or 'bad' model. There are clearly aspects of postmodernity that any Marxist will find alarming: the triumphant interpenetration of commodification and culture, for instance; which is to say, the way the dominant forms of art of the present day are also explicitly commodities – pop CDs and films, and their associated merchandising. But Jameson also acknowledges an excitement, a 'euphoria' (*P*: 32), a new intensity of experience that is opened up by the shiny surfaces of postmodern simulation.

Something else does tend to emerge in the most energetic postmodernist texts, and this is the sense that beyond all thematics or content the work seems somehow to tap the networks of the reproductive process and thereby to afford us some glimpse into a postmodern or technological sublime, whose power or authenticity is documented by the success of such works in evoking a whole new postmodern space in emergence around us.

(*P*: 37)

Jameson returns, at the end of his essay, to architecture as 'in this sense the privileged aesthetic language'. His account of a particular building in downtown Los Angeles – the Westin Bonaventure Hotel designed by postmodern architect John Portman – remains amongst the most famous, or at least widely-disseminated, pieces of his writing.

This enormous hotel stands in 'disjunction from the surrounding city' (*P*: 41) (Jameson appends a photograph to show us what he means), with its 'great reflective glass skin' which reflects and therefore 'repels the city outside' in the same way that somebody wearing reflective sunglasses 'repels' other people (*P*: 42). More crucially, its inside is designed without the usual reference points that make it easy for the individual to orient his or herself. Stepping inside the Bonaventure, Jameson attests, is a disorienting experience; great escalators and elevators move the subject around, but the space itself is fragmented and flattened.

> I am more at a loss when it comes to conveying the thing itself, the experience of space you undergo when you step off such allegorical devices [as the escalators] into the lobby or atrium, with its great central column surrounded by a miniature lake, the whole positioned between the four symmetrical residential towers...I am tempted to say that such space makes it impossible for us to use the language of volume or volumes any longer, since these are impossible to seize...you are in this hyperspace up to your eyes and body.
>
> (*P*: 42–3)

Jameson equates this three-dimensional experience with 'that suppression of depth I spoke of in postmodern painting or literature'; and depthlessness and a 'waning of the affect' made concrete. Jameson can even make a wry Marxist point: the space is so disorientating that it becomes very hard to navigate, and the various shops and boutiques contained in the atrium are almost impossible to reach, 'even if you once located the appropriate boutique, you would be most unlikely to be as fortunate a second time'. Accordingly, 'the commercial tenants are in despair and all the merchandising is marked down to bargain prices'. Jameson concludes: 'when you recall that Portman is a businessman as well as an architect and millionaire developer, an artist who is at one and the same time a capitalist in his own right, one cannot help but feel that here too something of a "return of the repressed" is involved' (P: 44). The inference is: the capitalists are tripped up by their own systems.

Jameson is being more or less flippant here, but there is a serious point as well. All this emptied out, depthless mirror surface *is* repressing something as far as Jameson is concerned: history has not actually been banished, it has merely been hidden away in a 'political unconscious' that is all the more difficult to access. But Freud was adamant that the repressed always returns, and 'reality' (or to be more accurate, the Lacanian 'Real') will reemerge. This is perhaps why Jameson then goes from the 'complacent and entertaining (although bewildering) leisure space' of the Bonaventure to something altogether more serious. He moves from an edifice of consumer capitalism to the destruction and loss of life of the Vietnam War, and in particular Michael Herr's acclaimed memoir of his time fighting in it, *Dispatches* (1978). Herr writes in a postmodern manner 'in the eclectic way his language impersonally fuses a whole range of contemporary collective idiolects, most notably rock language and black language'. He does this because 'this first terrible postmodernist war cannot be told in any of the traditional paradigms of the war-novel or movie' (P: 44). The adjective there, easy to miss or underplay – 'terrible' – is key. It might seem somehow impertinent to call an event that involved such massive human suffering and loss of life as the Vietnam war 'postmodern', although there are clearly ways in which we might think it as such. It lacked the cultural centrality of World War II – a war which involved the whole world in an ideology of 'Good (democracy) versus Evil (Hitler's fascism, the Holocaust)'; Vietnam was instead a geographically marginal conflict, a war flattened and emptied out to a basic layer of violence, mixed in with popular culture and TV, accompanied in many people's imagination by a soundtrack of 1960s pop-music. But the violence and death was not 'hyper-real' or 'simulated', it was real. The Marxist perspective anchors discussion of these various postmodern phenomena to a bedrock that is, in some sense, essential. Slice it wherever and whenever you like, human history folds over as mostly suffering for most people. Jameson's criticism never loses sight of this fact.

SUMMARY

We can conclude, then, with an itinerary of Jameson's stylistic pointers to 'the postmodern'.

- The coexistence of *aesthetic* and *political* logics.
- The erosion of the categories of 'high art' and 'popular culture', and in particular the eruption of the popular ('kitsch') into all levels of artistic production.
- A fragmenting, eclectic *schizophrenia* in place of the modernist unifying 'paranoia'
- *Pastiche* instead of parody; 'blank' quotation and the inhabiting of styles
- A new depthlessness, a flattening that includes (for instance) the *waning of the affect*.
- The loss of any organic consciousness of *history*.

Above all, Jameson stresses again and again that his conception of the postmodern 'is a historical rather than a merely stylistic one'.

> I cannot stress too greatly the radical distinction between a view for which the postmodern is one (optional) style among many others available and one which seeks to grasp it as the cultural dominant of the logic of late capitalism: the two approaches in fact generate two very different ways of conceptualizing the phenomenon as a whole: on the one hand, moral judgments...and, on the other, a genuinely dialectical attempt to think our present of time in History.

(*P*: 45–6)

The point here is to emphasise, once again, the continuities between this 'postmodern' Jameson and the earlier more obviously 'Marxist' Jameson. As this passage makes clear, Jameson refuses to relinquish his key Marxist theoretical tools: the centrality of history as the 'Real' that texts (even anti-historical postmodernist texts) actually articulate; a complexly reasoned Hegelian/Althusserian belief in the intimate relationship between culture and socio-economics; and above all a commitment to a 'genuinely dialectical' criticism.

7

JAMESON ON CINEMA

Signatures of the Visible and *The Geopolitical Aesthetic*

One of the more recent developments in Jameson's criticism is an interest in cinema. Throughout the 1980s and 1990s he was writing a great deal of film criticism, and this chapter deals with that aspect of his work. This interest in the more popular medium of cinema has developed, in part, from Jameson's engagement with the debates around postmodernism, and, in particular, his sense that the post-modern cultural logic sees a blending of 'high art' and 'popular cultural' categories. Nonetheless, the strategies Jameson deploys in his readings of film represent a series of continuities with his early pre-postmodernism writings. Although published in 1992, Jameson's first book on cinema (*Signatures of the Visible*) in fact collects writings from the late 1970s as well as the 1980s. *The Geopolitical Aesthetic* (1992) continues his explorations of 'the political unconscious' via film. One of the key focuses of Jameson's film criticism is an awareness of the ways film reproduces this political unconscious in an especially direct manner. His readings of Western, and more recently of Third World cinema, is acutely sensitive to the historical and cultural forces that determine the art.

SIGNATURES OF THE VISIBLE

It might be thought that a Marxist critic would be particularly wary of analysing cinema, and Hollywood cinema above all; of all the forms of artistic practice current today, cinema is far and away the most expensive, and a 'big' film can only be made if significant capital investment by the richest industries of late capitalism. Jameson anticipates precisely this objection., that 'commercial films...inevitably place their production under the control of multinational corporations'. This might 'make any genuinely political content in them unlikely', and in fact might 'ensure commercial film's vocation as a vehicle for ideological manipulation' (*SV*: 38). But, Jameson suggests, this is to read texts at the level of 'intention' rather than understanding the way the political unconscious of even the most expensive film will necessarily manifest itself.

> No doubt this is so, if we remain on the level of the intention of the filmmaker who is bound to be limited consciously or unconsciously by the objective situation. But it is to fail to reckon with the political content of daily life, with the political logic which is already inherent in the raw material with which the filmmaker must work: such political logic will then not manifest itself as an overt political message, nor will it transform the film into an unambiguous political statement. But it will certainly make for the emergence of profound formal contradictions.
>
> (*SV*: 38)

In other words, Jameson is at pains to read both the 'manifest' text and also the 'latent' political signification. Sidney Lumet's 1975 film *Dog Day Afternoon*, for instance, is a film that Jameson considers can be 'focused in two quite distinct ways which seem to yield two quite distinct narrative experiences' (*SV*: 41). On the surface it seems to be a film of a type common in American cinema that follows the adventures of an anti-hero and what Jameson rather dismissively calls 'a kind of self-pitying vision of alienation' (*SV*: 38) (Jameson is patronising because this sort of American post-war 'existentialism' seems to him a pale imitation of the more authentic existentialism of Sartre, with whom − of course − Jameson began his academic career). But as the film goes on 'something different begins to happen' (*SV*: 43). Frustrated outsider Sonny, played by Al Pacino, holds up a branch bank and takes hostages; but gradually the audience is encouraged to be sympathetic to his character. By going against our expectations, on a formal level, this film 'makes a powerful non-conceptual point' (*SV*:

51), and Sonny becomes an 'allegorical' representation of the individual facing the oppressive anonymity and power of 'the present multinational stage of monopoly capitalism' (*SV*: 50). Ranged against Sonny, in the heat of the afternoon outside, is a police lieutenant (who 'comes to incarnate the very helplessness and impotent agitation of the local power structure') and a more powerful FBI agent, whose face we never see – 'the very absence of his features becomes a sign and an expression of the presence/absence of corporate power in everyday lives, all-shaping and omnipotent and yet rarely accessible in figurable terms' (*SV*: 38).

Signatures of the Visible reads a number of films this way. Jean-Jacques Beneix's 1981 film *Diva*, for instance, is 'a political allegory, the expression of a collective or political unconscious' relevant to the political situation in France in the 1980s (*SV*: 59). It concerns an opera-loving mailman who obtains bootleg recordings of a famous black operatic diva, who has never made an official recording. The tapes get mixed up with some other recordings that could incriminate Parisian gangsters, and much of the film is taken up with chase sequences, including a motorbike chase through the Paris subway system. Jameson sees the film as embodying a coded reconciliation of political antagonists that right wing ideology prefers to separate out – for instance, between white and black, 'of which the Diva herself, an American black (played by opera singer Wilhelmena Fernandez) comes as an ultimate permutation' (*SV*: 59). In particular, it is the *style* of the film – it is slick, cool, elegant and fascinated with surfaces, particularly shiny surfaces – that was most remarked upon on its initial cinematic release. Jameson comments that '*Diva*'s very images themselves perpetuate this process' of ideological coding (*SV*: 60).

His reading of Kubrick's *The Shining* (1980) connects with some of the things we have dealt with in the last chapter about 'nostalgia'. Jameson, with his acute sense of how history shapes texts, is sensitive to the 'pastiche' sense of history we associate with postmodernism, what he here calls 'what is inauthentic about nostalgia films...the cult of the glossy image' (*SV*: 85). *The Shining*, though set in the present day, is inhabited by a 'nostalgic' sense of a lost American past, from the opening sequence of the film (which is an 'aerial tracking shot across quintessentially breathtaking and picture-postcard "unspoiled" American natural landscape') to the hotel at the centre of the film itself, 'whose old-time turn-of-the-century splendor is undermined by the more meretricious conception of "luxury" entertained by consumer society' (*SV*: 86). In *The Shining*, Jack Nicholson's lead character has the job of house-sitting this hotel in the closed season, with his wife and son. He goes mad, sees ghosts and is possessed by 'evil' of some description, eventually trying to murder his family. In other words, although Jameson sees this horror film as a 'reinvention' of the 'older sub-genre...the ghost story' (*SV*: 89), he links this 'manifest' text with what *really* haunts *The Shining* — the latent forces of history itself, distorted in the mock-nostalgia of the piece.

> The Jack Nicholson of *The Shining* is possessed neither by evil, as such, nor by the 'devil' or some analogous occult force, but rather simply by History, by the American past as it has left its sedimented traces in the corridors and dismembered suites of this monumental rabbit warren [the hotel].
>
> (*SV*: 90)

Signatures of the Visible also contains detailed readings of Alfred Hitchcock's films, and a detailed discussion of the ways 'realism' and anti-realism (such as 'magic realism' or other postmodern manifestations) impact upon his concern with the historical and political transcodings he sees in cinema today. His chapter on Hitchcock reviews a study by the film-critic William Rothman called *Hitchcock: the Murderous Gaze* (1982), which identifies Hitchcock's fascination with loners and outsiders, and goes on to argue that this mysterious figure, who has many incarnations in Hitchcock's films, is in fact a means by which Hitchcock can insert himself in his own films. Of Norman Bates, the psychotic murderer of the film *Psycho* (1960), Jameson comments:

> Norman, then, *is* Hitchcock...in particular the Outsider around whom so many of these films turn...proves to have been not merely the expression of a particular theme or obsession of aesthetic interest to Hitchcock, but more than that the very inscription of Hitchcock himself *within* the film.
>
> (*SV*: 120–1)

Jameson finds this critical interpretation 'elaborate and ingenious' and asserts that 'it would be frivolous to decide whether it is true or false' (*SV*: 123). But characteristically he suggests that it lacks a proper sense of the *history* and the *ideological mechanisms* by which film is received by its audiences.

> I think, however, that we must go further into the historical originality and structural peculiarity of the film-viewing process...a certain historical (and historicist) enrichment and complexification of [contemporary film criticism] might be achieved if the mediation of 'reification' were inserted.
>
> (*SV*: 124–6)

This, in a sense, is what Jameson brings to the business of film criticism. Where much contemporary writing on film uses models of 'seeing' and 'viewing', the power of the gaze and the organisation of images (which are clearly crucial for cinema/TV) derived ultimately from Freud, Jameson insists that Freud must be combined with Marx for a proper perspective to be achieved. That the 'codes of the public [Marxism] and the private [Freudianism]' need to be 'co-ordinated', and in particular that it needs to be understood that 'the emergence of "seeing" as a social dominant' is 'the necessary precondition for its strategic functions in psychoanalytic models of the unconscious' (*SV*: 126). In other words, Freud's theories are useful for reading films provided they are first placed in the larger social and ideological contexts identified by Marxism.

THE GEOPOLITICAL AESTHETIC

The bulk of the films in *Signatures of the Visible* are Western, and indeed Hollywood films, although one of the essays in that volume ('On Magic Realism in Film') looks at three films from Poland, Venezuela and Colombia. This is symptomatic of Jameson's increasing interest in global culture, examining cultural and artistic productions from what used, rather patronisingly, to be called 'the Third World'. *The Geopolitical Aesthetic* is largely concerned with films more or less unknown to Western audiences, films in particular from the Far East.

The subject of Jameson's *The Geopolitical Aesthetic* has become, if anything, more relevant since its publication in 1994: examples of what he calls 'the conspiratorial text' have proliferated in late 1990s culture, partly because of the increasing dissemination of the Internet (a resource much given to 'conspiracy theories'), but also in such TV/film texts as *The X-Files*. Jameson is interested in these sorts of text because he sees in them an attempt, partial and allegorical though it is, to represent the sort of Hegelian 'totality' in which everything is an aspect of the larger whole. The totality in question is the negative one of the global manifestation of late capitalism. Films like *The Parallax View* (1974), *Three Days of the Condor* (1975), *All the President's Men* (1976) or in a slightly different way *Videodrome* (1983) – to mention only the American films that Jameson discusses in this extremely wide-ranging study – all these films are about characters uncovering a covert 'conspiracy' that underlies ordinary life and which seems to have its tentacles everywhere. Reading for the latent rather than the manifest content of these films encourages Jameson to see them as attempts to represent 'in allegorical form' the 'world system' of late capitalism, a totality 'so vast that it cannot be encompassed by the natural and historically developed categories of perception with which human beings normally orient themselves' (*GA*: 2). It needs to be allegorical, he argues, because only an allegory can suggest the range and scope of the system; allegory 'allows the most random, minute or isolated' aspects to 'function as a figurative machinery'. It also links together the 'manifest' fragmentation and reification of contemporary living that Jameson had so trenchantly analysed in *Postmodernism* with the 'latent' totality of the world-system. In other words, *The Geopolitical Aesthetic* elaborates upon a similar ground to *The Political Unconscious* (in particular, see above p. 81). The 'partial subjects, fragmentary or schizoid constellations' we associate with postmodernism are focused in these sorts of texts on the totalising 'trends and forces in the world system...a new density of global management' (*GA*: 5). And Jameson is in no doubt as to the pertinence of these 'global' assumptions. The 'conspiratorial' text, he says

> whatever other messages it emits or implies, may also be taken to constitute an unconscious, collective effort at trying to figure out where we are and what landscapes and forces confront us in a late twentieth-century whose abominations are heightened by their concealment and bureaucratic impersonality. Conspiracy film takes a wild stab into the heart of all that.
>
> (*GA*: 3)

The mechanism by which these sorts of conspiratorial text manages this representation of the global total is 'cognitive mapping', a term Jameson uses in several of his books.

COGNITIVE MAPPING

In general psychology, 'cognitive mapping' refers to the mental patterns people construct as a means of apprehending the world around them. Jameson picks up the term more specifically from Kevin Lynch's 1960 book *The Image of the City* which, he suggests, 'taught us that the alienated city is above all a space in which people are unable to map (in their minds) either their own positions or the urban totality in which they find themselves' (*P*: 51). Accordingly the 'cognitive map' an inhabitant of Jersey City will have of the urban space in which he lives will not be 'mimetic' – will not straightforwardly represent the actual space. Instead, it will reflect the distortions and omissions of the individual's personal experience of living in such an alienated environment. Jameson finds this concept 'extraordinarily suggestive', particularly 'when projected outward onto some of the larger national and global spaces', as he looks at in *Postmodernism* and *The Geopolitical Aesthetic*. In particular, it suggests the way the individual orients his or herself in relation to the ideological global totality, a totality as enormous and ungraspable as the complete layout of New York is to an individual on the ground; cognitive mapping gives a handle on 'the great Althusserian (and Lacanian) redefinition of ideology as "the representation of the subject's *Imaginary* relationship to his or her *Real* conditions of existence". Surely this is exactly what the cognitive map is called upon to do in the narrower framework of daily life' (*P*: 51).

The films he analyses in *The Geopolitical Aesthetic* are, in other words, visualised cognitive maps of the global totality that is just beyond our grasp. According to Colin MacCabe, who wrote the introduction to this study, 'cognitive mapping' is one of the most important of Jameson's methodologies, because it is the one that brings together 'the political unconscious' and 'postmodernism':

> Cognitive mapping is the least articulated but also the most crucial of the Jamesonian categories. Crucial because it is the missing psychology of the political unconscious, the political edge of the historical analysis of post-modernism and the methodological justification of the Jamesonian undertaking.
>
> (*GA*: xiv)

This is quite a large claim, and one that can really only be made in the wake of Jameson's writings on postmodernism, because of their emphasis on the visual and spatial logics of our cultural dynamic. For MacCabe, cognitive mapping 'works as an intersection of the personal and the social' (*GA*: xiv). This strikes me as overplaying the significance of the strategy in Jameson's thought a little, but there is no doubt that he sees 'mapping' as one of the key formal techniques by which people make sense of their socio-political environment. 'We map our fellows in class terms day by day,' Jameson observes, 'and fantasize our current events in terms of larger mythic narratives' (*GA*: 3). This is emphasis on narrative we remember from *The Political Unconscious*, but Jameson's 'postmodern' broadening of perspectives have moved him beyond what he now calls the 'banal political unconscious' towards a more global elaboration of the same concept:

> what I will now call a geopolitical unconscious. This it is which now attempts to refashion national allegory into a conceptual instrument for grasping our new being-in-the-world.
>
> (*GA*: 3)

Running through *The Geopolitical Aesthetic*, as we might expect, is a repeated emphasis on totality, and in particular on the ways certain representations (particularly certain films) contain within them an allegorical or cognitively mapped apprehension of this totality. For instance, Jameson thinks the assassination of John F. Kennedy in 1963 remains 'the paradigmatic assassination in (Western) modern times', not because Kennedy himself was so significant ('in that respect, Malcolm X, or Martin Luther King, or Bobby Kennedy probably generated more intense experiences of mourning') but because of the sense experienced at the time that *this* assassination brought the whole of the USA together, generated a fleeting understanding of totality:

> the experience of the media, which for the first time and uniquely in its history bound together an enormous collectivity over several days and vouchsafed a glimpse into a Utopian public sphere which remained unrealized.
>
> (*GA*: 47)

In Britain, the spontaneous expressions of national mourning for the death of Diana, Princess of Wales, in 1998, which reached bizarre levels, had a similar effect. But it could be argued that the outpouring of grief at Diana's death has an added Jamesonian inflection, a more postmodern cultural logic. Kennedy's death had a structure of meaning underlying it, in the sense that Kennedy was the sitting president, a person of actual political power, whereas Diana was a simulacrum of a political figure, a quintessentially postmodern individual constituted by an economy of images in the sphere of popular culture.

That said, most of Jameson's examples are more postmodern than anything else. *The Geopolitical Aesthetic* contains a reading of Sidney Lumet's account of the Watergate conspiracy, *All The President's Men* (based on the first-person accounts of Bernstein and Woodward, the journalists who uncovered the governmental cover-up). Jameson observes how the film turns 'on information and representation rather than anything substantive – how to smear the Democrats in public view' (*GA*: 68). This emptying out of content, this flattening of representation, finds – Jameson would say, of course – itself particularly embodied on the *formal* level of the film. *All The President's Men* is a spy thriller, but it is one in which all the usual generic adventures of spy films (as Jameson offhandedly puts it, 'any number of villains, torture sequences, struggles, agons, kung fu or wrestling collisions' (*GA*: 69)), are absent. Jameson describes the effect of the film, which is fairly muted if powerful in oblique suggestiveness, as 'chamber music in the realm of melodrama' (*GA*: 68).

Towards the end of the book there is an attentive reading of a film by the Philippine director Tahimik, *The Perfumed Nightmare* (1977). In this film, set at the end of the 1960s, a Philippine man's enthusiasm for the USA's moon landing leads him to organise a Werner von Braun fan club. He is later able to travel to France, where his idealisation of the West is undermined by the sight of 'older markets being supplanted and destroyed by hideous concrete supermarkets'. He returns home disillusioned, and 'rememorates the martyrdom of his father, who was killed by American soldiers during their occupation of the Philippines' (*GA*: 190–1). Made while the Philippines were under the oppressive regime of the Marcoses, Jameson sees this film as transferring onto 'American imperialism' the unsayable problems of living in a dictatorship. But Jameson traces the 'geopolitical unconscious' of the film down to the most basic levels. The film contains, for instance, a series of shots of a little bridge in the Philippines. Jameson sees this visual image as a straightforward coding of the Marxist concept of 'mediation' (see above p. 78).

'Mediation', for example, is here symbolically designated by the picture of a bridge, and specifically of the little hump-back stones bridges of the village over which real and toy vehicles laboriously pass. As a 'concept' it has something to do with the relationships between cultural stages (Third and First worlds); between the [class] 'levels' of social life itself…between the past and the future…and between confinement and freedom.

(*GA*: 196)

This perhaps seems a little literalistic, even crude given the supple complexities of so much of Jameson's critical interpretations. Victor Burgin, in an excellent account of Jameson's book, notes the ways that the actual Freudian 'unconscious' is rarely so straightforward in its symbolism as bridge = mediation. Nonetheless, Jameson is adamant that 'this particular film has a message and seeks to transmit an ideological lesson of a type embarrassing if not inconceivable for First-World (realistic) film-makers'. What makes it unusual, Jameson thinks, is that this Marxist subtext is 'demonstrated on the First World rather than the Third' (*GA*: 204): that instead of a patronising Western perspective on the problems of the Third World we are given a dissection of 'the bourgeois epoch' as it manifests itself in Western society, from the perspective of a Philippine artist.

Jameson concludes his reading of *The Perfumed Nightmare*, and *The Geopolitical Aesthetic* as a whole, with a brief manifesto as to the task facing the critic.

One's sense, then, in the present conjuncture, sometimes called the onset of postmodernity or late capitalism, is that our most urgent task will be tirelessly to denounce the economic forms that have come for the moment to reign supreme and unchallenged. This is to say, for example, that those doctrines of reification and commodification which played a secondary role in the traditional or classical Marxian heritage, are now likely to come into their own and become the dominant instruments of analysis and struggle.

(*GA*: 212)

We have seen how crucial 'reification' and 'commodification' are to Jameson's Marxist analysis of contemporary culture. His writings on film extend these analyses, and point out the ways cinematic texts shape our sense of being-in-the-world (ideology) as well as providing means to unpick the mystifications of late capitalism.

SUMMARY

In general, then, the strengths of Jameson's work on cinema and TV reside in his insistence that a film needs to be read as a product of its particular historical and ideological circumstances. Postmodernism opens up the range of Jameson's critical analysis, but he engages with the predominantly psychoanalytical emphasis of much film criticism by reasserting his sense of the political unconscious – or his revised notion of a *geopolitical* unconscious, and a renewed insistence on the importance of reification and mediation as cultural processes.

AFTER JAMESON

Jameson's impact in the areas of Marxist literary criticism and post-modernism has been enormous; his theories have received enthusiastic endorsement from some and occasionally vitriolic attacks from others, but they continue to make waves in the worlds of criticism and theory.

JAMESON AND 'MTV MARXISM'

As we might expect, the fortunes of his particular project of Marxist analysis has been caught up in the broader historical and cultural fortunes of communism in the latter years of the twentieth century. For many people the collapse of the Berlin Wall and the changes in the former Soviet Union are understood as a more general discrediting of all the ideas associated with the name of Marx; and into this climate of opinion we see two things happening. On the one hand, some Marxist critics become more hard-line in their Marxist affiliations, insisting that Marxism has been discredited in the popular imagination because it has drifted too far from the true creed. On the other hand, there are critics whose work adapts Marx to the times. In Britain in the 1990s this drama was played out in the socialist Labour Party; old-school party members insisted that the party had been out of power for decades because it was insufficiently socialist, and modernisers struggled to create what they called 'New Labour', where the Marxist origins of the party were reconfigured to take account of the logics of contemporary capitalism (the modernisers, under Tony Blair, eventually won the day). We see something similar in the reputation of Fredric Jameson. The Marxist thinker Alex Callinicos has attacked much of Jamesonian postmodernism, amongst other things, in a book entitled *Against Postmodernism* (1989). Postmodernism is flawed and dangerous, Callinicos thinks, because it 'lacks a referent in the social world'. As far as Callinicos is concerned, Jameson has effectively sold out his Marxist beliefs by moving away from the belief in Marxism as a socially revolutionary mode of thinking. Old style Marxists still believe that a workers' revolution is the best way to overturn the evils of capitalism. Callinicos argues that 'postmodernism' represents a turning away from that revolutionary ideal, as well as being a depressing symptom of our fallen age.

> Socialist revolution is the outcome of historical process at work throughout the present century...Postmodernity by contrast is merely a theoretical construct, of interest primarily as a symptom of the current mood of the Western intelligentsia...Not only does belief in a postmodern epoch usually go along with rejection of socialist revolution as either feasible or desirable, but it is the perceived failure of revolution which has helped to gain widespread acceptance of this belief.
>
> (Callinicos 1989: 1)

In slightly gentler mood, Terry Eagleton chides Jameson as representing the 'academicisation' of what for earlier Marxists 'had been a mode of political intervention'. Eagleton insists this is not 'a cheap gibe at armchair Marxists' and concedes that 'it is preferable for radical ideas to survive in an armchair than to go under altogether', but it is hard to shake the sense that Jameson is blamed not merely for abstaining from revolutionary social intervention himself, but for writing criticism that discourages others from believing in revolution (Eagleton and Milne 1996: 12).

Other Marxist critics have seen in Jameson's versions of Marxism the chance to breath new life into that system of belief. Perry Anderson admits that 'in the past, Jameson's writing was sometimes taxed with being insufficiently engaged with the real world of material conflicts – class struggles and national risings – and so held "unpolitical". That was always a misreading of this unwaveringly committed thinker' (Anderson 1998: 136). For Anderson, Jameson is central to the revivification of left-wing political thought, in part, precisely because his anatomy of the current condition of culture, postmodernism, has been so precise and incisive.

A younger critic, Clint Burnham, is even more unashamedly enthusiastic about the impact Jameson has had. 'I cannot remember *not* having read Jameson', he declares, so ubiquitous has Jameson's work been in his own intellectual development (Burnham 1995: 243). According to Burnham, Jameson has created something he calls 'MTV Marxism': a hip, trendy new Marxism that encompasses popular culture as well as hard theoretical writing. 'MTV Marxism' means more than that Jameson's postmodernism sees the demotic, popular models of culture as paradigmatic; it has to do with the excitement with which Jameson's work has been received in some quarters.

> I would argue that many intellectuals of my generation read the work of Jameson...as mass culture; by my generation I suppose I mean those born in the late-fifties or sixties...My point is that in this milieu, Jameson [is] on the same plane as Shabba Ranks and PJ Harvey and *Deep Space Nine* and John Woo: cultural signifiers of which one is a much as 'fan' as a 'critic'.'
>
> (Burnham 1995: 244)

'MTV Marxism', as its name suggests, is posited as a more mass-market, popular form of Marxism than the more desiccated forms associated with other theorists.

JAMESONIAN POSTMODERNISM

As this suggests, it is Jameson's interventions in the debates surrounding postmodernity that have had the most profound and most recent impacts on the debates of theory in the west. In particular, Jamesonian ideas of postmodernity as the populist, fractured cultural logic of late capitalism have generated a great deal of debate; and his distinction between 'parody' and 'pastiche' has been taken up by many other theorists. In Perry Anderson's uncharacteristically colourful phrase: 'exploding like so many magnesium flares in the night sky, Fredric Jameson's writings have lit up the shrouded landscape of the postmodern' (*CT*: xi). As we saw in Chapter 6, there have been a great many conflicting critical interpretations of what postmodernism even is, but generally speaking there are two readings of the logic of contemporary culture. One is a Lyotardian or Hassanian postmodernism, which sees postmodern art as a continuation of modernism, as characterised by a rather austere avant-garde aesthetic of resistance and fragmentation. On the other hand there is the Jamesonian postmodernism that Chapter 6 examined, which sees contemporary culture in other terms: as an eruption of a the popular into the arena of high art which is energetic and exciting as well as being in some senses problematic; as the expression of a very particular social and economic set of circumstances rather than a trans-historical cultural style. It is fair to say, I think, that the Jamesonian postmodernism is the more widely cited and employed one; whole areas of study, particularly the burgeoning academic fields of Cultural Studies and Media Arts, draw on Jameson's insights into the way postmodernism is an energetically popular phenomenon. One of the most influential strategies of reading that Jameson established is the one that sees useful resistances and radical value in texts other critics might dismiss as crudely ideological or complicit with the system. We saw how he was able to find interesting things to say about even so right-wing a writer as Wyndham Lewis in *Fables of Aggression*. Similarly, he is able to read populist films like *Jaws* and *The Godfather* in radical ways, since there is a 'transcendent' element in 'even the most degraded type of mass culture' which is able to be 'negative and critical of the social order from which, as a product and commodity, it springs' (*SV*: 29). Certainly Jameson's writings on postmodernism have been extremely influential across a wide range of disciplines, and it is not possible to enter into the debates surrounding that term without taking account of what Jameson has to say.

JAMESON AND 'THIRD WORLD STUDIES'

Jameson's more recent writings have received various forms of criticism. In particular, his writings in the 1990s elaborated a perspective on world literature; he has undertaken subtle and penetrating readings of films by the Indonesian director Kidlat Tahimik, of Chinese poet Lu Xun, and of the status of what he calls 'Third World' literature and culture. This expansion of Jameson's critical attentions outside the narrow canons of Western art and literature has been welcomed by many; and is itself part of a broader shift in 1980s and 1990s criticism towards what is sometimes called 'post-colonial culture', the cultures of Africa, Asia and South America. Jameson's own high profile, and his Marxist affiliations, have given his writings in this field a particular impact, but at the same time there are some who are unhappy with this most recent development in Jameson's work.

The critic Aijaz Ahmad has taken issue with Jameson's work in this area. He finds it 'awkward' to criticise Jameson: 'if I were to name the *one* literary critic/theorist writing in the USA today whose work I generally hold in the highest regard it would surely be Jameson'. Nonetheless, Ahmad finds something reductive in Jameson's desire to reduce the heterogeneity of world literature to a single label 'Third World'.

> I have been reading Jameson's work now for roughly fifteen years...and because I am a Marxist, I had always thought of us, Jameson and myself, as birds of the same feather, even though we never quite flocked together. But then, when I was on the fifth page of this text [Jameson's 1986 essay 'Third World Literature in the era of Multinational Capital'] (specifically, on the sentence starting 'All third world texts are necessarily...' etc.), I realised that what was being theorized was, among many other things, myself. Now, I was born in India and I write poetry in Urdu, a language not commonly understood among US intellectuals. So I said to myself: '*All?...necessarily?*'.
>
> (Ahmad in Eagleton and Milne 1996. 95)

Ahmad finds Jameson's division of the world into 'First World' and 'Third World' reductive, and ultimately to reproduce the oppressive strategies of defining the 'Third World' inhabitants in terms of their *otherness* to a First World norm. He also finds Jameson's work narrowly gendered ('it is inconceivable to me', he says, 'that *this* text could have been written by a US *woman*') and also racially marked ('it is equally inconceivable to me that *this* text could have been written by a Black writer in the USA').

Jameson would not deny his own historical and cultural specificity; he is a white male, part of an affluent group of Western intellectuals in today's world. Indeed, understanding the historical and cultural context, the unconscious of Jameson's own texts, should be the first strategy we, as readers, undertake when we pick up one of his books. But the claim that he, unconsciously or otherwise, tries to reduce the variety and range of Third World literatures to a monolithic unitary determination is a more damning one. Satya P. Mohanty agrees with Aijaz Ahmad, and finds this weakness in Jameson's writing 'indeed ironic', precisely because so much of Jameson's earlier work (books like *The Political Unconscious*) were so aware of the complex and various forces at work in Western literature. 'Why, then,' Mohanty asks, 'is Jameson so quick to see...third world cultures...in such reductively utopian or abstract terms?' (Mohanty 1997: 113). His answer to his own question is that there is a flaw in Jameson's underlying philosophical approach; that, putting it roughly, Jameson's attachment to the Marxist notions of totality undermines his ability to allow for the heterogeneity of world literatures. His work 'cannot account for such a complex variety...since all such variety is subsumed into the Althusserian opposition between science and ideology'.

Jameson remains the world's most famous American Marxist thinker; and his commitment to the principle of the dialectic means that he presumably welcomes engagement in debate by critics such as Mohanty and Ahmad. His Marxist readings of literature and especially narrative, his subtle engagements with other Marxists thinkers and critics, and his powerful combination of Marxism and Freud continue to inspire and excite. More widely influential, he is the single most significant critic to have defined and explored 'postmodernity', the cultural logic of the age in which we are all still living.

FURTHER READING

WORKS BY FREDRIC JAMESON

This study has looked at most of the important books and essays written by Jameson from the 1970s to the present day. References to these works are abbreviated in the text as follows:

CT   *The Cultural Turn: Selected Writings on the Postmodern 1983–1998* (1998)

FA   *Fables of Aggression: Wyndham Lewis, the Modernist as Fascist* (1979)

GA   *The Geopolitical Aesthetic: Cinema and Space in the World System* (1992)

IT1   *The Ideologies of Theory, Essays 1971–1986* vol. 1 (1988)

IT2   *The Ideologies of Theory, Essays 1971–1986* vol. 2 (1988)

LM   *Late Marxism: Adorno, or the Persistence of the Dialectic* (1990)

M&F   *Marxism and Form* (1971)

P   *Postmodernism, or The Cultural Logic of Late Capitalism* (1991)

PHL   *The Prison-House of Language* (1972)

PU   *The Political Unconscious* (1981)

SV   *Signatures of the Visible* (1990)

Fuller publication details for Jameson's major works are given below:

—— (1961) *Sartre:The Origins of a Style*, 2nd edn, NewYork: Columbia University Press, 1984.

A study of the French writer and philosopher Jean-Paul Sartre, which began as Jameson's PhD thesis.

—— (1971) *Marxism and Form: Twentieth Century Dialectical Theories of Literature*, Princeton: Princeton University Press.

A sophisticated introduction to the work of a number of Marxist thinkers including Theodor Adorno, Walter Benjamin, Herbert Marcuse, Ernst Bloch, Georg Lukacs and Jean-Paul Sartre. Jameson also uses this intellectual context to develop his own theories about the importance of Marxist analysis of the *form*, as opposed to the content, of literary works.

—— (1972) *The Prison-House of Language: A Critical Account of Structuralism and Russian Formalism*, Princeton: Princeton University Press.

Explores the ideas associated with the structuralist schools of criticism, particularly Claude Levi-Strauss, Roman Jakobson, Ferdinand de Saussure and Roland Barthes. As a Marxist, Jameson criticises structuralism in several regards.

—— (1979) *Fables of Aggression:Wyndham Lewis, the Modernist as Fascist*, Berkeley: University of California Press.

Subtle reading of the right-wing modernist writer Wyndham Lewis from a left-wing point of view that reads 'against the grain' to recover interesting and useful things from the sexism and racism of Lewis's novels.

—— (1981) *The Political Unconscious: Narrative as a Socially Symbolic Act*, London and NewYork: Routledge.

Classic account of 'narrative' as a key formal element in Marxist analysis that seeks to synthesise Marxist and Freudian perspectives into a powerful critical methodology.

—— (1988) *The Ideologies of Theory, Essays 1971–1986*, Minneapolis: University of Minneapolis Press (2 vols: 'Theories and History of Literature vols 48 and 49').

Jameson's major essays collected into two volumes; includes celebrated essays on Utopia, 'Of Islands and Trenches', on 'Periodizing the 1960s' and the title essay 'The Ideology of Theory'.

—— (1990) *Late Marxism: Adorno, or, The Persistence of the Dialectic*, London: Verso.

A detailed and complex reading of the work of Frankfurt School Marxist philosopher Theodor Adorno, which concentrates in particular upon his 'negative dialectical' philosophical method.

—— (1990) *Signatures of the Visible*, New York and London: Routledge.

Collection of previously published essays on a wide range of films, including *Godfather*, *Dog Day Afternoon*, *Diva*, *The Shining*, and many others.

—— (1991) *Postmodernism, or, The Cultural Logic of Late Capitalism*, London: Verso.

This volume reprints Jameson's famous defining essay 'Postmodernism, or the Cultural Logic of Late Capitalism' as its first chapter, and augments it with a large number of other essays on related themes published by Jameson over the 1980s.

—— (1992) *The Geopolitical Aesthetic: Cinema and Space in the World System*, Bloomington: Indiana University Press.

Jameson's second book on cinema develops an argument about the way films represent the paranoia prompted by the world system of Late Capitalism with films fascinated with conspiracy such as *Videodrome*, *Three Days of the Condor* and *The Parallax View*.

—— (1994) *The Seeds of Time*, New York: Columbia University Press.

Originally a series of lectures delivered at the University of California, this elegant book examines the logics of contemporary postmodern culture and the problem of Utopia.

—— (1998) *Brecht and Method,* London: Verso.

A study of the connections between Brecht's drama and his politics which argues that Brecht's method was a multi-layered process of reflection and self-reflection, reference and self-reference.

—— (1998) *The Cultural Turn: Selected Writings on the Postmodern 1983–1998*, London: Verso.

Another collection of essays previously published elsewhere, including 'The Antinomies of Postmodernism' (which is also a chapter in *The Seeds of Time*).

WORKS ON FREDRIC JAMESON

FURTHER READING ABOUT MARXIST LITERARY CRITICISM AND POSTMODERNISM

If you want to find out more about Marxism and Marxist Literary Criticism, a good place to begin is the anthology of writing edited by Terry Eagleton and Drew Milne, *Marxist Literary Theory* (Oxford: Blackwell, 1996). This gives a good spread of representative writers from Marx to the present day, and covers both general Marxist theory and the literary-critical aspects of Marxist thinking.

There are a great many accounts of postmodernism. Two can be particularly recommended as first stops: Perry Anderson's *The Origin of Postmodernity* (London: Verso 1998) began life as an introduction to *The Cultural Turn*, the selection of Jameson's writings on postmodernity. Anderson gives both an excellent short (136 pages) account of the phenomenon, and also provides detailed and useful readings of a range of Jameson's work. Hans Bertens, *The Idea of the Postmodern* (London: Routledge, 1995) is more wide-ranging, and more questioning, if not quite as elegant as Anderson's account.

FURTHER READING ON JAMESON

The following books are all useful for what they have to say about more specific aspects of Jameson's works:

Burgin, Victor (1996) *In/Different Spaces: Place and Memory in Visual Culture*, Berkeley: University of California Press, pp. 194–211.

A useful reading of *The Geopolitical Aesthetic*, as part of a powerful examination of the way images function in contemporary society.

Burnham, Clint (1995) *The Jamesonian Unconscious: The Aesthetics of Marxist Theory*, Durham: Duke University Press.

Trendy and intellectually restless jog through the whole of Jameson's career; sometimes a little fidgety, but fun and stimulating.

Dowling, William C. (1984) *Jameson, Althusser, Marx: An Introduction to The Political Unconscious*, Ithaca: Cornell University Press.

A little dry in places, but this remains the standard introduction to *The Political Unconscious*, an extremely clear and useful point of entry to that book.

Eagleton, Terry (1986) *Against the Grain: Essays 1975–1985*, London: Verso.

Contains two chapters that engage in a debate with Jameson's Marxism: 'The Idealism of American Criticism' (pp. 49–64) and 'Fredric Jameson: the Politics of Style' (pp. 65–78). Eagleton is sympathetic to Jameson's project, but comes out of a rather different school of Marxist thinking himself.

Goldstein, Philip (1990) *The Politics of Literary Theory: An Introduction to Marxist Criticism*, Tallahasse: Florida State University Press.

Very thorough and sober-minded account of contemporary Marxist criticism. His account of 'The Marxism of Fredric Jameson' is part of his chapter on 'The Politics of Reading' (pp. 146–61).

Homer, Sean (1998) *Fredric Jameson: Marxism, Hermeneutics, Postmodernism* (Key Contemporary Thinkers Series), New York: Routledge.

Up-to-date introduction to the range of Jameson's thinking, with a useful perspective on the postmodern.

Kellner, Douglas (1989) *Postmodernism / Jameson / Critique* (PostModern-Positions 4), Washington: Maisonneuve.

This volume contains a wide range of essays on Jameson, with a particular emphasis on the ways in which his interest in postmodernism can be reconciled with his lifelong interest in a Marxist 'totality' of approach.

Schwab, Gabriele (1993) 'The subject of the political unconscious' in Mark Poster (ed.), *Politics, Theory and Contemporary Culture*, New York: Columbia University Press, pp. 83–110.

Sensitive account of Jameson's *The Political Unconscious*, stressing its strengths but also aware of the gaps in his approach, particularly the way questions of 'women and gender' get obscured.

Of the books listed above, the best ones to begin with are probably Homer, Goldstein and Anderson. There are also a number of issues of journals devoted to Jameson:

Diacritics (Fall 1982), 12(3). Special issue on *The Political Unconscious*.
New Orleans Review (Spring 1984), 11(1).

INTERNET RESOURCES

For a detailed book list of work on Jameson, go to:
http://sun3.lib.uci.edu/indiv/scctr/Wellek/jameson/index.html

WORKS CITED

Note: Works by Fredric Jameson which are cited in this book are listed in the Further Reading section.

Adorno, Theodor (1990) *Negative Dialectics* (Trans. E.B. Ashton), London: Routledge.

Althusser, Louis (1972) *Lenin and Philosophy and Other Essays*, London: Monthly Review Press.

Anderson, Perry (1998) *The Origin of Postmodernity*, London: Verso.

Bennington, Geoffrey (1994) 'Not yet', in *Legislations: the Politics of Deconstruction*, London: Verso, pp. 71–87.

Bertens, Hans (1995) *The Idea of the Postmodern: A History*, London: Routledge.

Burgin, Victor (1996) *In/Different Spaces: Place and Memory in Visual Culture*, Berkeley: University of California Press, pp. 194–211.

Burnham, Clint (1995) *The Jamesonian Unconscious: The Aesthetics of Marxist Theory*, Durham: Duke University Press.

Callinicos, Alex (1989) *Against Postmodernism: A Marxist Critique*, Cambridge: Polity.

Dowling, William C. (1984) *Jameson, Althusser, Marx: An Introduction to The Political Unconscious*, Ithaca: Cornell University Press.

Eagleton, Terry (1986) *Against the Grain: Essays 1975–1985*, London: Verso.

Eagleton, Terry (1991) *Ideology: An Introduction*, London: Verso.

Eagleton, Terry and Milne, Drew (1996) *Marxist Literary Theory*, Oxford: Blackwell.

Forgacs, David (1995) 'The politics of modernism', in Maroula Joannou and David Margolies (eds) *Heart of a Heartless World: Essays in Cultural Resistance in Memory of Margot Heinemann*, London: Pluto Press, pp. 8–18.

Freud, Sigmund (1995) *The Freud Reader*, ed. Peter Gay, London: Vintage.

Goldstein, Philip (1990) *The Politics of Literary Theory: An Introduction to Marxist Criticism*, Tallahassee: Florida State University Press.

Hassan, Ihab (1971) *The Dismemberment of Orpheus: Towards a Postmodern Literature*, New York: Oxford University Press.

Hegel, Georg (1988) *The Hegel Reader*, ed. Stephen Houlgate, Oxford: Blackwell.

Hemling, Steven (1996) 'Jameson's Lacan', *Postmodern Culture* 7(1) September (http://mvse.jhv.edu/Journals/postmodern_culture/toc/pmc7.1.html)

Kellner, Douglas (1989) *Postmodernism/Jameson/Critique*, PostModernPositions 4, Washington: Maisonneuve.

Lacan, Jacques (1977) *Ecrits: a Selection* (Transl. Alan Sheridan), London: Tavistock.

Lacan, Jacques (1979) *The Four Fundamental Concepts of Psycho-Analysis* (Trans. Alan Sheridan), Harmondsworth: Penguin.

LaCapra, Dominick (1985) *History and Criticism*, Ithaca NY: Cornell University Press.

Lewis, Wyndham (1968) [1918] *Tarr*, London: Jupiter Books.

Marx, Karl (1983) *The Portable Karl Marx*, London: Penguin/Viking.

Mohanty, Satya (1997) *Literary Theory and the Claims of History: Postmodernism, Objectivity, Multicultural Politics*, Ithaca: Cornell University Press.

Nicholls, Peter (1995) *Modernisms: a Literary Guide*, London: Macmillan.

Schwab, Gabriele (1993) 'The subject of the political unconscious' in Mark Poster (ed.) *Politics, Theory and Contemporary Culture*, New York: Columbia University Press, pp. 83–110.

Seldon, Raman (1985) *A Reader's Guide to Contemporary Literary Theory*, Brighton: Harvester Press.

Zizek, Slavoj (1993) *Tarrying with the Negative: Kant, Hegel and the Critique of Ideology*, Durham: Duke University Press.

INDEX

Note: References in **bold type** identify where the author or text concerned is quoted.